MODERN WORLD NATIONS

MODERN WORLD NATIONS

Bolivia

Mandy Lineback Gritzner

and

Jason M. Gritzner

Series Consulting Editor
Charles F. Gritzner
South Dakota State University

CHELSEA HOUSE
PUBLISHERS
A Haights Cross Communications Company

Philadelphia

Frontispiece: Flag of Bolivia

Cover: Adobe houses on Lake Titicaca.

CHELSEA HOUSE PUBLISHERS

VP, NEW PRODUCT DEVELOPMENT Sally Cheney
DIRECTOR OF PRODUCTION Kim Shinners
CREATIVE MANAGER Takeshi Takahashi
MANUFACTURING MANAGER Diann Grasse

Staff for BOLIVIA

EXECUTIVE EDITOR Lee Marcott
PRODUCTION ASSISTANT Megan Emery
PICTURE RESEARCHER 21st Century Publishing and Communications, Inc.
SERIES DESIGNER Takeshi Takahashi
COVER DESIGNER Keith Trego
LAYOUT 21st Century Publishing and Communications, Inc.

A Haights Cross Communications ◀ Company

http://www.chelseahouse.com

First Printing

1 3 5 7 9 8 6 4 2

Library of Congress Cataloging-in-Publication Data applied for.

ISBN 0-7910-7481-1

MODERN WORLD NATIONS

Table of Contents

Bolivia

The Aymara are a strong ethnic group who live in dwellings such as this one in the La Paz region of the Andes Mountains.

Introducing Bolivia: An Unusual Land

B olivia is a very peculiar place. It is a land whose sights, sounds, and smells will challenge your reality and haunt your memories. Bolivia is a place where llama fetuses are sold by street vendors and live sheep are taken to market strapped to the roofs of taxis. Locals delight in spending a Sunday drinking a brew of fermented corn juice, and many proclaim that sitting on a hot rock causes sickness! Bolivia is also a country whose natural wonders stretch from towering ice-clad mountain peaks to steamy tropical jungles. And it is a land whose culture and history are both clearly visible, and whose people are proud, gracious, giving, and friendly.

Bolivia lies at the heart of the South American continent and therefore embodies much of what is "South American." In an area about the size of Texas, Oklahoma, and Kansas combined, you will find incredible diversity. There are pines and palm trees, donkeys and

Mercedes Benzs, stone huts and modern city towers, poor subsistence farmers and millionaires. In some places, you can see all this diversity in a single city block!

When flying into La Paz, Bolivia's capital, a visitor immediately recognizes that this city is unique. The La Paz airport, perched on the edge of the Altiplano, a high plateau, is a staggering 13,100 feet (3,993 meters) above sea level. In fact, visitors often stagger a bit as a result of *soroche,* the altitude sickness that is experienced by many foreigners at this elevation. The view of La Paz from the rim of the Altiplano is truly one of the world's most striking urban sights. The huge city sprawls along and up the sides of a narrow valley some 1,650 feet (503 meters) below, backed by the magnificent snow-capped peaks of the Cordillera Real. The highest, Illimani, reaches a glacier-clad elevation of 21,184 feet (6,458 meters).

Along the steep streets of La Paz, which is Bolivia's bustling economic center, you will see many kinds of people. Native women, called *cholitas,* dress in ample skirts with numerous petticoats and wear bowler-style hats. They share the same streets with contemporary businesswomen wearing Western-style attire. Visitors will see people selling all wares imaginable — from *charangos,* or tiny stringed instruments sometimes made of armadillo shell, to fossils, to watch batteries. Anything one may need can be found in La Paz, and every *casera* (salesperson) wants you to buy something. It is difficult to walk down a narrow, winding street without someone calling out through a giant smile, "*¿Que vas a llevar, hoy día?*" — "What are you going to carry (buy) today?"

Visitors to Bolivia surely would not want to miss a trip to sparkling Titicaca, the huge lake located just north of La Paz. Bolivia shares the shores of this amazing lake with Peru. It is such a popular destination that even many Bolivians, who normally don't travel, have been to *El Lago* (The Lake). Lake Titicaca has at least two claims to fame. It is the highest navigable lake in the world, and the Incas declared Isla del Sol, an island in the middle of the lake, as the birthplace of the sun. Certainly Isla de Sol, or "Island of the Sun," was a tremendously important location to the Incan Empire. Citizens farmed, raised llamas, and made sacrifices to the gods on the island. Ceremonial altars can still be seen there today, and it is considered a very sacred site by many Andean people.

Bolivia is normally considered to be "Andean" because the most populated part of the country lies in the Andes Mountains. More than two-thirds of Bolivia, however, is lowland tropical plains. This area of steamy jungles and flat savanna stretches all the way from the eastern slope of the Andes to the Brazilian border and is a paradise of biodiversity. In fact, parts of tropical Bolivia contain more species of birds, animals, plants, and insects per square mile than anywhere else on earth. In all, geographers recognize at least 13 distinct ecological zones in Bolivia—making it an incredibly diverse land. Sadly, corrupt and often merciless logging companies target these tropical areas for exploitation.

The people of Bolivia cannot be considered wholly "Andean" either. The highland dwellers are mostly indigenous (native) people, either Quechua or Aymara, the two most populous ethnic groups in the country. The Aymara were living near Lake Titicaca before the Incas arrived, while the Quechua are believed to be descendents of the Inca Empire. The Guaraní, an indigenous group living in the lowlands, number about 20,000 and speak their own language. There are also *Afro-Bolivianos* (African Bolivians) living in the Yungas cloud-forest region near La Paz and *Japonés-Bolivianos* (Japanese Bolivians) living in Okinawa, a tropical town named for the Japanese island.

Historically, Bolivia has been famous (or perhaps infamous, depending on your view) for its mining. When the Spanish conquered present-day Bolivia in the 1500s, many of the indigenous people, who were once part of the great Inca Empire, were enslaved and put to work in the Spanish-held tin, gold, and

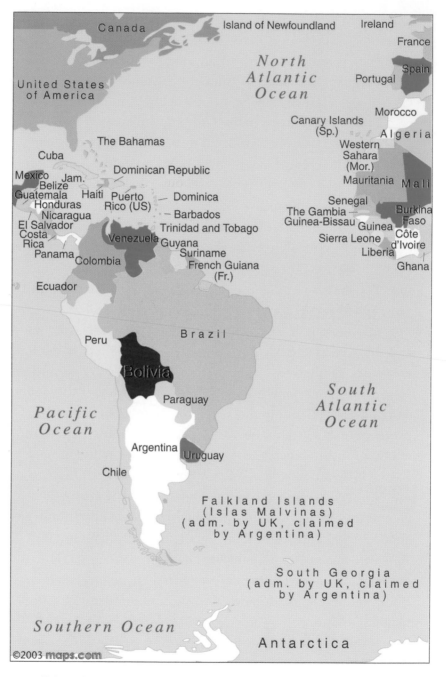

Bolivia is located in the heart of the South American continent.
It is considered an Andean country because it lies partly in the
Andes Mountains.

silver mines. The Bolivian workers were often mistreated by the Spanish and worked in subhuman conditions for many hours or even days at a time. According to one tale, enough gold was mined in Bolivia to build a golden bridge from the country all the way to Spain. Even today, so much resentment exists in Bolivia toward Spain that many people claim to speak the language *castellano*, meaning "Castilian," named for a major region in Spain, rather than *español,* or "Spanish."

Today, mining contributes only about 10 percent to Bolivia's GDP (gross domestic product). This section of the economy, however, is expected to see future renewal and growth. Petroleum, rather than metals, now provides the government with its largest single source of income. If the exploration of gas reserves continues at its projected rate, revenues are expected to triple in the next decade.

Although the petroleum industry contributes most to the GDP, tourism and the timber industry of the tropics are also generous providers of revenue to the country's economy. Agriculture, however, is the sector of the economy that employs the most people. Although farming contributes only about 16 percent to the GDP, it employs more than one-third of the country's work force.

Historically, Bolivia's good fortune with natural resources has not been matched by good luck in war. While today Bolivia has a landmass of 424,164 square miles (1,098,580 square kilometers), its area was much larger in the past. In just over 100 years following its declaration of independence from Spain, Bolivia had lost more than half of its original territory in wars with Chile (1879–84), Brazil (1903), and Paraguay (1938). The worst defeat occurred when Bolivia lost its outlet to the Pacific Ocean to Chile, making it a landlocked country and isolating it commercially. Many Bolivians continue to feel bitter over the loss. Today, however, the country is able to transport its products by land to Argentina and Peru, and from there by water to markets including the United States.

One product making its way north from Bolivia, despite its landlocked status, is the illegal drug cocaine. In reality, very little cocaine is manufactured in Bolivia, but the country is a large grower of coca, the plant used for making cocaine. Though coca is used to produce cocaine, the leaves are less harmful when chewed, and Bolivians have chewed the leaves for centuries. People there use coca medicinally to cure stomach pain, toothaches, and altitude sickness. Traditionally, elders have "read" coca leaves to tell one's future and put them in ritual fires for good luck. Coca's use dates back to the Incas, perhaps in the late fifteenth century if not before. Now coca is used mostly by subsistence farmers, who refer to it as the *la hoja sagrada*, the sacred leaf.

The United States used to import coca leaves for use in many pharmaceuticals, but more notably for the production of a refreshing and invigorating tonic, Coca-Cola. While the leaf is still imported for use in some prescription medicines, the Coca-Cola company now uses only flavoring from the leaf, not the "active" ingredients, to create its drink's trademark taste.

Despite coca's widespread sacred status in Bolivia, the United States Drug Enforcement Agency (DEA), in an attempt to reduce production of cocaine, has been working in conjunction with the Bolivian government since 1987 to eradicate coca. *Cocaleros*, or coca farmers, have protested the program since it began and have even won some small battles against the government's laws. The general consensus is, however, that the *cocaleros* are fighting a losing battle, and that one day coca may disappear entirely.

Although Bolivia is a beautiful and fascinating nation, it has many problems. Perhaps this is why it is one of South America's least known countries. Poverty is perhaps the major problem affecting the country's people today. Ninety-seven percent of the rural population is considered to live below the poverty level. High inflation rates and the lowest personal income in South America plague the nation and only make the poor standard of living more extreme. The entire country suffers economically and many people, including those with a college education, are underemployed or unemployed.

Bolivia also has a history of corrupt government rule. The corruption has not improved the lives of the mostly indigenous population, and many Indians remain uneducated and illiterate. Though the government has helped provide Bolivia's cities with electricity, paved roads, telephones, and even Internet service, many of the rural areas lack these modern amenities. Most Bolivians blame the government for these conditions, and civil unrest brought on increasing water prices, coca eradication efforts, and economic inflation often occurs.

Today, there are indications that more people are learning about Bolivia. The tourist industry, for example, is growing as many travelers visit this spectacular land and its varied people. Butch Cassidy and the Sundance Kid did just that back in 1907, when they learned about the riches of Bolivia and ventured there to share in the spoils (even though they weren't willing to work for the treasure). Before settling down to a planned quiet lifestyle of ranching in the tropical lowlands near Santa Cruz, the two robbed a mining company of $90,000. Unfortunately, their dreams were denied. Near the high, dry, cold Salar de Uyuni, they took their own lives rather than die in a gunfight during an unsuccessful getaway.

The story of Bolivia is a long and fascinating tale. It dates back millions of years to a time before the mighty Andes themselves were formed. Today the story of Bolivia continues. ¡Vamos a Bolivia!

At 21,462 feet (6,542 meters) Mount Sajama is Bolivia's tallest mountain and one of the highest volcanoes of South America.

2

Bolivia's Natural Environment

O ne cannot understand or appreciate Bolivia without consider-
ing the impact of its natural environment. Bolivia offers a
rich variety of environmental conditions that present both
splendid opportunities and severe challenges. Through time, people
have learned to use the land and its resources in many different ways.
Physical geography plays a role in where people live, what they do, what
natural resources are available for their use, and what hardships they
must overcome. Using the land and its resources, people also change the
environment in many ways. In this chapter, you will learn about
Bolivia's natural endowment—its land features, weather and climate,
plant and animal life, and natural resources.

DIVERSE LAND FEATURES

Bolivia borders five other countries, and its boundary measures

3,780 miles (6,083 kilometers). Its neighbors are Peru to the northwest, Chile to the southwest, Brazil to the north and east, Paraguay to the southeast, and Argentina to the south. The country lies wholly between the equator and the Tropic of Capricorn (23.5 degrees South).

In Bolivia, the Andes Mountains are at their widest. They run north-south as two main parallel ranges, or *cordilleras*, occupying the western half of the country. The westernmost range, the Cordillera Occidental, roughly follows the Peruvian and Chilean borders. To the east, the Cordillera Oriental stretches from Peru to Argentina. The Andes divide Bolivia into three geographic zones: the rugged and towering mountains and high plateau of the Altiplano in the west; the semitropical Yungas and temperate valleys of the eastern mountain slopes; and the tropical lowlands, or Oriente, that occupy roughly the eastern two-thirds of Bolivia.

Mountains and Altiplano

The Andes range is young geologically speaking. In fact, its formation continues today, as earthquakes and active volcanoes continue to push the mountains higher and higher. These earthquakes and volcanic eruptions occur as the mighty Nazca plate in the Pacific Ocean collides with and dives under the continental South American plate. As the Nazca plate is driven down into the earth's hot interior, it melts and forms magma that rises to the surface as scorching lava in a string of volcanoes called the Cordillera Occidental on the border with Chile. Here, Bolivia's highest peak, the snowcapped Sajama, reaches 21,420 feet (6,529 meters). Sajama and Payachatas (at 20,800 feet, or 6,340 meters) are the only two peaks in the western cordillera that are snow-covered throughout the year.

Further to the east, the Cordillera Oriental has been thrust skyward for thousands of feet in a series of folds and faults. Between the two ranges lies the sprawling Altiplano, a high plateau over which tower the steep slopes of even higher mountain peaks.

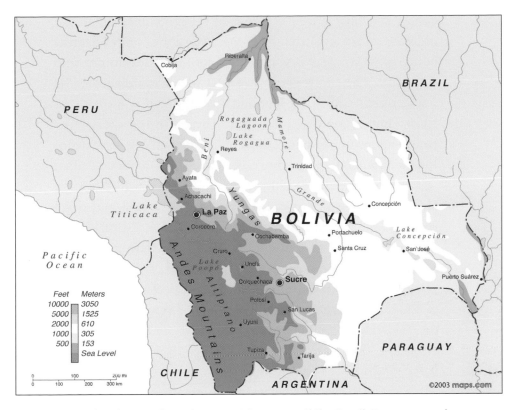

Bolivia borders on five other countries: Peru, Chile, Brazil, Paraguay, and Argentina. In Bolivia, the Andes Mountains are at their widest. Two parallel ranges, or *cordilleras*, run along the western side of the country.

The southern half of the Cordillera Occidental receives very little precipitation and hence has hardly any vegetation. Here the landscape consists mainly of barren rocks, mineral deposits, and lava flows. The northern half of the cordillera receives just enough moisture to support a ground cover of scrubby vegetation. One area receives just enough rainfall to sustain one of the highest forests in the world—a forest of crooked and scrubby *kewiña* trees that ring the lower slopes of Sajama. Virtually all of the Cordillera Occidental is sparsely populated, but the southern section is almost uninhabited.

The other major mountain range in Bolivia is the more

eastern and older Cordillera Oriental. It begins at the north end of Lake Titicaca and extends southeastward to about 17 degrees South latitude where it widens and continues southward into Argentina. The more impressive part of this cordillera is the northern half, called the Cordillera Real, which is made up of snow-capped granitic mountains. These are the spectacular peaks that people often recall when picturing Bolivia. Many of the mountain crests rise above 20,000 feet (6,100 meters). Two of the most notable are Illimani (21,184 feet, or 6,458 meters), located at the southern end of the Cordillera Real and over-looking La Paz, and Illampu (21,076 feet, or 6,424 meters) at the northern end of the cordillera. Both of these peaks and many others in the range have upper slopes in the icy grip of glaciers. Because of the many high ice-clad peaks in this section of the Cordillera Oriental, Bolivia is sometimes referred to as the "Nepal of South America." Nepal, of course, lies in the Himalaya Mountains on the Eurasian continent and contains some of the highest mountains in the world, including Mt. Everest, the world's highest.

South of Lake Titicaca, the Cordillera Oriental takes on a very different appearance than in the north. This southern section is called the Cordillera Central, a range of mountains formed by a massive block of the earth's crust that has been thrust upward in a series of folds and faults. The mountains here may appear less impressive, because there are no snow-capped peaks, but elevations still reach upward of 17,000 feet (5,182 meters) in places and the range features many steep cliffs and deep valleys.

The Bolivian Altiplano is normally thought of as a vast flat tableland between the Cordillera Occidental and the Cordillera Oriental. In actuality, it is more complex, with isolated upland areas dividing the region into four major drainage basins. The Altiplano stretches over 560 miles (900 kilometers) from south-ern Peru to northern Argentina, occupying about 10 percent of Bolivia's area. The eastern side of the Altiplano is a broad, continuous, flat area, where the principal north-south transportation route through the country has been located since colonial times.

Originally, before it became a high plain, the Altiplano was a deep valley lying between two great mountain ranges. During the Tertiary period (between 65 and 1.8 million years ago), the rift was gradually filled with debris that eroded (washed down) from the mountains. This deposition could explain why the Altiplano slopes from north to south. More rainfall and glacial action in the north resulted in greater erosion and deposition of sedimentary debris here than in the south.

Much of the Altiplano lies at around 11,500 to 13,150 feet (3,505 to 4,008 meters). Because it is located on the leeward (downwind) side of the mountains that first encounter major weather systems from the humid eastern lowlands, it is said to be in the "rain shadow" of the Cordillera Oriental. The Altiplano therefore receives very little direct precipitation. It is almost a barren desert, practically devoid of trees. Winds can be strong on the Altiplano, stirring up dust clouds and making the already cold air even more bone chilling. Most of the time, however, the air is clear and the sky is blue.

The Altiplano region contains several salt flats, which are dried-up remains of ancient lakes. Its Salar de Uyuni is the highest and largest salt lake in the world, located at an elevation of 11,975 feet (3,650 meters) and covering over 3,475 square miles (9,000 square kilometers). During the dry season, Uyuni is bone dry; in fact, its parched lake bed even serves as a transportation route that time of year. During the wet season, however, the basin fills to become a vast inland sea, twice as large as Utah's Great Salt Lake. Salt deposits on the lake bed range in depth from 6 to 65 feet (2 to 20 meters) and during the dry season the surface is a blinding white. Algae in the region's other saline lakes create unusual colors, as in Laguna Colorado (bright red), or Laguna Verde (neon green).

The salt flats experience extreme ranges of temperature.

The Salar de Uyuni is the highest and largest salt lake in the world. During the dry season it has no water and is a huge salt flat. It draws tourists from all over and, in fact, has a hotel that is created entirely of salt.

Temperatures of 86°F (30°C) have been recorded at midday and −13°F (−25°C) the following midnight! A trip across the Salar is a trip through the surreal. Cactus-covered rocky islands rise out of an ocean of salt, and pink flamingos (remember, this place is normally very cold) bathe in technicolor lakes. Traveling across the Salar, one can even stay in a famous hotel built entirely of salt—including the beds, tables, and chairs!

Although the Salar is an amazing physical feature, the most prominent and best-known feature on the Altiplano is Lake Titicaca. Found at the northern end of the high plain at an elevation of 12,500 feet (3,810 meters), Titicaca is the highest navigable lake in the world and is also the largest in South America (not counting Venezuela's Lake Maracaibo, which actually is an arm of the ocean). This spectacular lake covers an area of 3,205 square miles (8,300 square kilometers) and its average depth is over 330 feet (100 meters), with the deepest point measured at 922 feet (281 meters). Bolivia's border with Peru passes through the middle of the lake, with each country claiming about half of the water body.

At least 25 different rivers flow into Lake Titicaca, mostly from mountain snowmelt and precipitation in Peru. A slow-moving, reed-filled river called the Desaguadero flows southward toward Lake Uru Uru and Lake Poopó, 155 miles (250 kilometers) away, draining the lake. This sluggish outlet removes only about 5 percent of the total river flow into the lake; the rest is lost to evaporation. Therefore, the waters of the lake are slightly brackish (salty), creating prime conditions for the growth of *totora* reeds, which are found growing along the banks of the lake. The reeds are used by local residents to make mats and reed boats for which the region is famous.

Unlike the waters of Lake Titicaca, Lake Poopó is salty and shallow, with depths rarely more than 13 feet (4 meters). Poopó's size varies throughout the year, since it is completely dependent on seasonal rainfall and the overflow from Lake Titicaca for its water. In times past, the lake has dried up when rainfall was low or when the Desaguadero River silted up so its flow could not reach Lake Poopó. In years of heavy rainfall, though, Lake Poopó has overflowed to the west, filling another of the salt flats, the Salar de Coipasa, with shallow water.

All three lakes—Titicaca, Uru Uru, and Poopó—were joined during the last ice age to form a vast inland water body called Lake Ballivián. This lake stretched at least 370 miles (595 kilometers) south from Lake Titicaca and included the Salar de Uyuni as well as the Salar de Coipasa. Lake Ballivián's water levels were much higher than those of the current lakes in the area. The level of Lake Ballivián is estimated to have been more than 330 feet (100 meters) above the present level of Lake Titicaca and 740 feet (226 meters) above the level of Lake Poopó.

Yungas and Valleys

East of the Cordillera Real, land drops away toward the Amazon Basin into the deeply cut, lush green valleys of the *Yungas*. Here, warm, moist, westward-moving air from over the Amazon Basin backs up as it reaches the towering Andean barrier. As the air moves upslope, the moisture condenses into clouds that shroud the upper reaches of these valleys, creating cloud forests. Abundant precipitation provides ample moisture to support the growth of the dense forests, fruit trees, coffee, and coca that grow in the rich soils of the Yungas.

Transportation problems, however, have historically hindered agricultural trade and development in the Yungas. Beginning in 1917, the Bolivian government attempted to build a railroad from La Paz into the eastern lowlands, but the construction was so difficult that the project was abandoned after completion of only 93 miles (150 kilometers). Today, to arrive in the quaint town of Coroico, located in the Nor Yungas (North Yungas), it is necessary to brave what has been labeled "the most dangerous road in the world." This terrifying one-lane mud road winds its way along 1,000-foot-high cliffs (305 meters) without guard rails. In some places, waterfalls tumble down and cross the road itself. It is no wonder the "Yungas Road" has one of the highest fatality rates in Bolivia. At the most frightening turns and drop-offs, simple wooden crosses have been placed by family members to remind drivers of loved ones who died there. A few tour companies have recently sprung up in La Paz to capture the market on what is probably the safest mode of travel down this winding wet route: mountain bikes!

South of the Yungas and east of the Cordillera Central, the slopes again descend steeply toward the east to form a series of sharp valleys and ridges. The rivers that drain these mountains eastward have cut long narrow valleys through the countryside. These valleys, warmer than the Altiplano but cooler than the eastern lowlands, are important locations for both farming and human settlement. With valley floors at around 6,500 to 10,000 feet (2,000 to 3,000 meters), a wide range of agricultural possibilities exist, including the all-important corn (maize). This crop traditionally is used to make offerings to the gods during celebrations, but it is also the main ingredient in the production of *chicha*, the local alcoholic brew.

Perhaps the two most important Bolivian valleys are Cochabamba and Cliza. Today, both are very densely populated and are referred to as the "Breadbasket of Bolivia," because the cropland is so fertile. The largest city in the area is Cochabamba, with a population of 517,000. The valley areas of Bolivia stretch to the south all the way to Tarija, Bolivia's southernmost major city.

The valley region is, in some respects, the most geographically diverse part of the country. Although it is often overlooked as an attraction because it does not wholly contain either the Altiplano or the tropical lowlands, it touches both of these regions and encompasses all the environments that lie between. Because it lacks extremes, many Bolivians believe that the valley region is the country's best and most comfortable area.

Eastern Lowlands

Bolivia's eastern lowland plains occupy about 70 percent of the country's area. This hot and humid lowland region spreads north and east from the Andean foothills and Yungas. The area is much more sparsely populated than the Altiplano or Yungas and associated valleys. Until recently, the lowlands played a minor role in Bolivia's economy. The recent discovery of rich petroleum and natural gas reserves, however, has brought great attention and considerable development to this region.

Topographic and climatic differences separate the lowlands into three distinct subregions. The northern area, which consists of the Beni and Pando Departments ("departments" are administrative land areas similar to states in the United States) and the northern section of the Cochabamba Department, is mostly flat and consists of true tropical rain forest. Here, giant trees form a canopy that shades the ground from sunlight, so that much of the animal and bird life is found in the treetops. The topsoil in the region sits on a layer of hard clay and therefore drainage is very poor. In fact, if rains are heavy, the rain forest often becomes a massive swamp.

Although the lush rain forest vegetation would suggest otherwise, soils here are notoriously poor. The warm tropical climate and high precipitation lead to strong weathering of the soils. Additionally, minerals and other nutrients are continuously leached (washed from the soil by rainwater) from the upper layers, and at any point in time, most nutrients are not in the region's soils but in the vegetation. As trees and other plants die, their nutrients are returned to the soil in a continuous natural cycle. From these leached soils, however, do come some valuable products, including rubber trees, quinine (a substance used to treat malaria), mahogany (a tropical hardwood), cashews, and Brazil nuts.

The second lowland subregion, the central area, consists of the northern half of the Santa Cruz Department. This section receives less rain than the northern lowlands and has gently rolling hills. Here, dry deciduous forest alternates with tropical savanna or tropical steppe, both of which contain scrub brush and grasses. Much of the land, however, has been cleared for cultivation or grazing purposes.

If rainfall came to this area year-round, the savannas likely would be covered by dense tropical forest, but here precipitation comes only in extremes. During the annual rainy season, drainage is so poor that shallow floods often cover much of the land. This time of year, cattle can starve for lack of vegetation. Transportation during the rainy season can be nearly impossible, even with the most efficient vehicle. In the dry season, however,

During the rainy season the savanna lands can become covered with a shallow layer of water that will support plants such as these water lilies.

the land is so dry and scorched that many people have to purchase water from merchants who bring it from nearby rivers.

The largest city in the lowlands, Santa Cruz de la Sierra (normally called just Santa Cruz), is found in this region, as are most of the country's natural gas and petroleum reserves. Santa Cruz lies in a wooded location at an elevation of around 1,500 feet (457 meters) and has an average yearly rainfall of 45 to 60 inches (114 to 152 centimeters). Very close to the city lie large tracts of fertile and well-drained soils that produce tropical and semitropical fruits, cotton, rice, oils, and sugarcane.

East of the city of Santa Cruz, the land begins to descend gradually to around 300 feet (91 meters) above sea level at the Brazilian border. Natural grasslands, low vegetation, and cattle are found in this area, but most of the land still remains unused. Although the region is good for ranching, inadequate transportation limits the accessibility to markets, especially during the rainy season.

The third lowland subregion is called the Chaco, a semi-arid area that extends into Paraguay. Here, virtually no rain falls during nine months of the year. However, during the brief season of heavy precipitation, much of the area becomes a vast, soggy, swampland. The variation in rainfall supports only thorny scrub vegetation browsed upon by a few scraggly herds of goats and cattle that are able to eke out a meager existence in this tough environment. The greatest attractions in the Chaco region are the approximately 170 million barrels of recoverable oil reserves and 3 trillion cubic feet of natural gas, both recently discovered. Some new settlers have decided the extremes in climate are worth the effort to help exploit these resources.

WEATHER AND CLIMATE

Weather and climate are two very important components of any natural environment. Weather refers to the day-to-day conditions of the atmosphere, whereas climate is the long-term (usually 30 years or more) average of weather conditions. These two factors, combined with land features, are the primary forces affecting the natural vegetation, wildlife habitat, and water systems of the world. Weather and climate also are of great importance to land use and other human activities.

The two most important elements of weather and climate are temperature and precipitation. The two primary factors affecting these elements in Bolivia are wind systems and elevation. The latitudinal zone in which Bolivia is located is home to the trade wind system, part of a global circulation pattern. There are two trade wind belts—one north of the equator called the Northeast Trades, and one south of the equator called the Southeast Trades. (Winds are always named by the direction *from* which they blow.) Of the two, the Northeast Trades bring a summer rainy season to much of Bolivia as they push moisture from the Amazon Basin toward the interior. As the warm, moist air rises over the mountain ranges, the air cools and condenses its moisture. This process is called *orographic* uplift.

During Bolivia's winter, or low-sun period, the dominant winds lessen and little moisture is drawn over the country. Nevertheless, some random precipitation can occur year-round in the northern section of the country as far west as Lake Titicaca, where the Northeast Trades continue to bring some occasional moisture.

Bolivia's northern lowlands have a wet tropical climate with high temperatures, high humidity, and heavy rainfall year-round. The daytime high temperatures average around 86°F (30°C) all year in most parts of this region. The climate of the central lowland areas is considered tropical wet and dry, or savanna. During the summer (October to April in the Southern Hemisphere), the Northeast Trades ply this region with hot, humid, rainy weather. In the winter months (May to September), the Southeast Trades predominate and precipitation is minimal. Because the winter days and nights are normally clear, temperature extremes are greater than during the rainy season. However, these average tropical conditions can be interrupted by cold winds that blow into this area from the south. These winds, called *surazos*, can cause cold, rainy weather that may last as long as a week, leaving even the monkeys shivering in their leafy perches!

The Chaco region has a semiarid steppe climate. Here, the rainy season lasts only from January to March as the Northeast Trades take some time to push south before bringing hot and humid conditions. From April to December, the

Chaco experiences dry weather with hot days and cooler nights. Bolivia's record high temperature, 16.6° F (47°C), was recorded in this region during the dry season.

In the valley and mountain areas, temperature and precipitation vary depending on elevation. The Yungas area is the cloudiest and most humid valley area because here the Northeast Trades push up against the high mountains, where their moisture is condensed through cooling. Up to 60 inches (152 centimeters) of rain falls here annually. Valleys and basins throughout the Cordillera Oriental, somewhat shaded from the full front of the Northeast Trades, have mostly mild temperatures and moderate rainfall, averaging about 25 to 30 inches (64 to 76 centimeters) per year. Temperatures decrease with increasing elevation at about 3.6 degrees Fahrenheit per 1,000 feet (1 degree Celsius per 1,000 meters). In the valleys and mountains, snowfall can occur above 6,500 feet (1,980 meters) and the permanent snow line is at around 15,000 feet (4,600 meters). Mountain areas over 18,000 feet (5,500 meters) have a polar climate and may include glaciers.

In the Altiplano, the Northeast Trades hardly affect the climate. Once winds cross the Cordillera Oriental, they lose most of their moisture. Therefore, there is no regular source of rainfall for the Altiplano. Strong cold winds, cloudless skies, and normally dry, cool weather mark the climate. Temperature here is primarily a function of elevation. Sharp differences occur between day and nighttime temperatures because of the altitude and absence of cloud cover. Average high temperatures during the day range from 60° to 70°F (16° to 21°C), but with no clouds to hold the warm air near the earth's surface, nighttime temperatures can fall to 5°F (−15°C).

PLANT AND ANIMAL LIFE

Bolivia is one of the world's greatest regions of biological diversity. Plant and wildlife species found nowhere else in the world make Bolivia's tropical rain forest and savanna their home. The highlands, although containing much less flora and fauna, also host some interesting and unlikely creatures.

Lowlands

Bolivia's lowland forests are situated between 10° and 15° South latitude and below 800 feet (244 meters) in elevation. Most of these areas lie within the Amazon Basin. The forests appear to be in pristine condition, but the reality is that they have been decimated by years of mahogany and South American cedar extraction, latex tapping, Brazil nut gathering, and present-day mining. These activities, coupled with hunting, have had a definite impact on the region's animal life, particularly the large mammals.

Usually, the best places to observe wildlife in the tropics are along the rivers. Caiman, which are large crocodile-like reptiles, and turtles are abundant. Squirrel monkeys and brown capuchin monkeys travel in large families, swinging from limb to limb to their destinations. Elusive sloths cling to high limbs and move so slowly that mold can grow on their matted fur! Peccaries, or black wild pigs, are rarely seen, but scratched ground indicating their presence can be commonly observed. A vast number of armadillos, deer, jaguar, and ostrich-like rheas also roam the lowland areas.

The capybara is an interesting rodent in this region. This huge animal, which resembles a guinea pig mixed with hippopotamus, is the world's largest rodent. It can stretch to more than 3 feet (.9 meters) in length and weigh more than 110 pounds (50 kilograms). These impressively sized rodents live in large groups and can often be seen feeding on lush grasses along riverbanks.

Another strange-looking mammal that can be found in some of the Amazonian tributaries is the pink dolphin. Myths surround this odd creature. One tale describes an underwater city where the dolphins walk on streets made of turtle shells and lie in hammocks consisting of anaconda.

The capybara is the world's largest rodent. It lives in large groups and can be seen swimming in or feeding on the lush grasses around Bolivia's rivers.

People believe the dolphin can take on a human form dressed in a white linen suit. Another tale says the dolphin can be a malevolent, spiteful creature if hunted, and killing one is equal to killing a powerful witch doctor, which always results in a terrible fate for the murderer.

In addition to the plentiful mammal, reptile, and amphibian life, fish here also are impressive. The Amazon Basin is home to perhaps 2,000 species, including piranha, stingray, and electric eel. Local people fish for a giant catfish, the *surubi*, in these waters. These catfish and many other edible fish provide an important source of protein for local diets. The bird species of the lowland regions are also numerous, including macaws, parrots, and toucans. Over 200 species of butterflies and count-less insect species also call the tropics their home.

Plant species of the tropical rain forest are innumerable. In fact, in Bolivia's national parks and reserves can be found some of the world's most diverse and abundant plant life. It is estimated that an area consisting of 0.75 square miles (2 square kilometers) of rain forest may have more than 1,200 species of vascular plants (those with specialized cells that conduct water and synthesize food, such as ferns), 600 species of trees, and 120 species of woody plants!

Many of the lowland forest trees have buttresses, or thick-ened portions of their trunks, that reach from the ground to some 10 to 12 feet (3 to 4 meters) up the trunk. Buttresses, it is believed, help support tall trees from falling over, as a high groundwater table doesn't allow roots to penetrate very deeply. Some smaller trees may have long thin prop roots that also extend up the side of the tree. Woody vines, called lianas, are very common and climb high into the tops of the trees. The lianas tangle themselves within the canopy and actually compete with the trees for space and light. Some of the more prolific vines will eventually kill the trees that they ensnare. Epiphytes, or plants that grow on or cling to a host but are not parasitic, are found on many of the lowland trees. These include lichens, mosses, orchids, ferns, and bromeliads.

Savanna

Savannas grow in sharp contrast to Bolivia's tropical rain forest. The savanna experiences both very wet and very dry seasons. With the onset of summer (November to December) rains, a season of new growth begins each year. Wildlife is similar to that of the tropics, and fish, macaws and other birds, giant anacondas, caiman, capybara, and swamp deer are commonly found here. It is usually easier to view wildlife in the savanna, because they frequently congregate around water sources.

Plant life of the savanna is comprised of mostly tall grasses and low shrubs. These areas are easily flooded during the rainy season, but small isolated sections of dry deciduous forest can be found.

Highlands

Plant and animal life of the Bolivian highland areas differ greatly from that of the lowlands and savanna. Vegetation is sparse. The low temperatures and dry climate support the growth of only shrubs, cacti, and dry grasses.

Animals are limited to those that can withstand the cold temperatures and thin air of the mountains and Altiplano. These include vicuñas (camelids, or camel-like mammals) and vizcachas (a small animal similar in appearance to a marmot crossed with a rabbit and that lives in rocky outcrops). There are also rheas (large, ostrich-like birds) and Andean wild cats. One unusual exception, mentioned earlier, is found in the salt flats area of the Altiplano, where volcanic vents warm a vast lake called Laguna Colorado. Here, huge flocks of pink flamingos and thousands of other water birds are able to survive. Imagine how odd it would be to see tropical pink flamingos at such a high elevation on the cold dry Altiplano!

NATURAL RESOURCES

Bolivia is rich in natural resources, especially timber, petroleum, natural gas, and minerals. The people of the country count on these resources for their economic exchange, but many of the resources are rapidly disappearing.

Vast timber resources are found in the tropical lowlands of Bolivia, and hundreds of tree species are good for commercial timber. Unfortunately, too many of these trees are logged illegally every year and sent mostly to Brazil, where they are then distributed worldwide. The region has to contend with deforestation and associated erosion caused by the widespread logging, which is a major threat to biological diversity.

Oil resources in Bolivia are found in the Santa Cruz Department, while natural gas is located in both the Santa Cruz and Tarija Departments. Exploration for petroleum and natural gas is growing rapidly. Bolivia plans to build numerous pipelines to more quickly move the gas to points of export. The country already exports gas to Argentina, and pipelines to Brazil and Paraguay are planned.

Bolivia's mineral resources include tin, antimony, bismuth, silver, lead, zinc, and gold. It also has large reserves of potassium, lithium, and iron. Gold is one of the leading earners of hard cash for Bolivia, and the gold mine near the town of Oruro produces over 14 tons of the precious metal a year. Traditionally, silver and tin have been mined in the Potosí Department, but companies are now beginning to look west toward the Cordillera Occidental and east toward the Brazilian border for unexploited mineral reserves. A huge iron ore deposit, perhaps one of the world's largest, already has been found near the Brazilian border.

Lake Titicaca is the highest navigable lake in the world. It has long been a
major population center for Bolivians and the cultures that predated them.
Today it is a major tourist destination.

3

Early History

BOLIVIA'S FIRST INHABITANTS (7000 B.C. – 500 B.C.)

Bolivia's physical geography has impacted its cultural history since the dawn of settlement in this rugged region. Even though it lies near the equator, Bolivia shares very few similarities with the region's tropics. In this geographically diverse nation, most people have always settled in higher, cooler zones located between 5,000 and 13,000 feet (1,524 to 3,963 meters). The most advanced cultures in Bolivia's history chose to live at bone-chilling elevations of 12,000 feet (3,658 meters) or higher. So do most of the country's people today. While Bolivia's highlands are not totally inhospitable to humans, they do have poorer soils, as well as drier and colder climates, than the lowlands.

Historically, the climatic differences between the high country and the lowlands required the domestication of plants and animals unique to both environments. Conditions in the highlands also had an impact on human evolution. Humans had to physically adapt to the limited supply of oxygen and lower air pressures at the high elevations. The hearts and lungs of mountain people, for example, are larger than those of lowlanders.

There has been much speculation about the earliest human history of Bolivia. Archaeologists (scientists who study early humans) now believe that many important cultural advances, and especially developments in agriculture, occurred on the barren, windswept Altiplano, the highest plateau in Latin America. Artifacts found on the Altiplano place the first humans in the area at around 7000–8000 B.C.

How did the first inhabitants arrive in the Andes? It was long believed that Asian immigrants crossed the Bering Strait region and gradually moved southward into what is now South America toward the end of the Ice Age. Today, some scientists believe that a coastal or even an all-water route may have been taken by the first human settlers in the Americas. A secondary migration may have occurred from the tropical valleys and lowlands on the eastern side of the Andes up to the Altiplano. This type of migration can help to explain why Bolivia's indigenous ("Indian") people look almost Asian in appearance.

The earliest people to live on Bolivia's Altiplano followed a seasonal cycle of hunting and gathering near the shores of Lake Titicaca. The lake, with its 3,500-square-mile (9,065-square-kilometer) surface area, influences the local climate, providing humidity and relative warmth not found in other locations on the Altiplano. The eastern half of the Altiplano also has reasonably fertile soils and vast mineral deposits. There is evidence to suggest that groups of people surrounding the lake began to participate in intensive agriculture and herding around 3,000 B.C. These activities provided an essential food surplus to help families survive the long dry winters on the high plateau.

ANIMAL DOMESTICATION

The Bolivian Altiplano seems to be an important center of domestication in South America. Many of the basic products of Andean civilization were developed near the shores of Lake Titicaca, including the potato, a crop that later had a great impact on the populations of Europe. Because root crops could be frozen and dehydrated in the cold, dry air of the Altiplano, they have been essential staples in the Bolivian diet for centuries. A number of other nutritional crops, including the high-protein grain quinoa, were also domesticated in the area. Today, quinoa is becoming popular in the United States. Its nutritional value is becoming well known and many people are using it rather than rice in many dishes.

The Altiplano was also the location for the domestication of the American camelids, or camel-like animals, such as the llama, alpaca, and vicuña. This development coincided with advances in farming. The llama was especially important to the Andean people, as it provided a much-needed protein source for the local diet as well as wool for weaving warm garments for the cold climate. The camelids were also used on farms as beasts of burden and their manure as sources of fertilizer and fuel for heating. This combination of the domestication of the camelids and the development of farming helped encourage the rise of the great Andean civilizations. Permanent settled communities, more complex social organization, and increased population density became common. The size of urban centers grew, and religious ceremonial areas followed. These advances also marked the beginnings of tradesmen who provided services to the full-time agriculturalists.

THE TIAHUANACO EMPIRE (500–1200 A.D.)

Expansion by the Aymara-speaking Indians of the Altiplano between about 500 and 900 A.D. resulted in the increasing power and influence of the Tiahuanaco (or Tiwanaku) culture.

Their ceremonial center, also called Tiahuanaco, located on the southeastern shores of Lake Titicaca, was a considerable development in Bolivian history. It was also the southernmost of the pre-Columbian Andean empires. The Tiahuanaco Empire was not completely confined to the Altiplano. It also inhabited small enclaves in other ecological zones spread from the eastern valleys of present-day Bolivia to the Pacific Coast. The settlement called Tiahuanaco is situated at an elevation of 13,120 feet (4,000 meters) and was at one time the religious and political center of the Altiplano, with over 50,000 residents. The community was agriculturally advanced. It also used pottery and metal objects dating from 100 A.D. onward. These advancements likely contributed to the rise of the better-known Inca Empire that followed the Tiahuanaco.

The Tiahuanaco Empire expanded rapidly after 1000 A.D., occupying nearly half of present-day Bolivia and parts of Chile, Peru, and Argentina. Sophisticated agricultural systems produced a surplus of crops, which gave the empire extra time and energy to raise large armies in order to conquer other Andean peoples. The armies conquered so many areas, in fact, that its engineers built an extensive system of paved roads through deserts and rain forests and over high mountain passes. These roads allowed the empire to maintain a constant flow of goods and information to all of its regions.

Great palaces, religious temples, and pyramids existed throughout the ancient city of Tiahuanaco. Community members built these impressive structures using blocks of stone that were carried on reed boats from quarries across Lake Titicaca. Each block weighed more than 150 tons. Buildings were usually intricately decorated with stone carvings, which were then covered with thin gold plates, or painted blue, red, gold, or black.

Despite all its many outstanding human and engineering feats, perhaps the most impressive Tiahuanacan development was the system of raised field agriculture. American anthropologist Alan Kolata believes that the engineering and building of

This reed boat carries a nine-ton boulder that was loaded on board using ancient methods of levers and ramps. It is set to sail across Lake Titicaca toward the ruins at Tiahuanaco to demonstrate that this method could have been used by the Tiahuanacan empire to build their large stone structures.

the fields, along with their bountiful production of crops, was unsurpassed among the world's farming peoples. Kolata found that one valley, cultivated by the Tiahuanacans using their specialized terraced fields, produced enough food to support over 125,000 people. Today, with the expert farming knowledge of these peoples gone, the same valley can barely support 7,000 people living in poverty!

Raised fields were necessary to overcome such environmental hardships as floods, droughts, infertile soils, and salinization from the slightly salty waters of Lake Titicaca. Tiahuanaco's engineers

These terraces are located on the Isla del Sol in the middle of Lake Titicaca. Valleys that were cultivated by the Tiahuanacans using terraced fields were able to produce enough food to support a large population.

and builders worked so many years to design and construct the terraces that many still exist today. The structures are immense, normally about 3 feet (1 meter) high and as much as 650 feet (200 meters) long and 50 feet (15 meters) wide. Deeply cut irrigation channels run alongside the fields, which lie parallel to one another. The advanced nature of Tiahuanaco's agricultural system, along with the riches gleaned from its conquered lands, likely helped the empire survive and prosper for many years.

Sometime after 1200 A.D., the Tiahuanaco Empire disappeared. One theory speculates that the civilization declined as a result of a drop in the level of Lake Titicaca, which left the lakeside city too far from the shore. Another theory proposes that Tiahuanaco was conquered and its people killed by the warring

Aymara from the west. The exact reason for the empire's downfall remains a mystery. It is known, however, that Tiahuanaco was the longest-lasting Andean empire in history and a perfect example of a great imperial capital.

AYMARA KINGDOMS (1100–1500 A.D.)

After the fall of Tiahuanaco, many different groups of Aymara people began to control the extensive territory left by the great empire. These Aymara cultures dominated the central highlands of Bolivia from the end of the twelfth century until the Spanish arrived in the sixteenth century. The Aymara lifestyle was distinctly different from the previous Tiahuanaco culture. Remember that the Tiahuanaco concentrated their towns along the lakeshore in open communities and practiced a highly productive terraced agriculture. The Aymara instead created hilltop towns behind forts away from the lake and intensely developed llama, alpaca, and vicuña herding. Whereas the Tiahuanaco had large temples and palaces for centralized religious ceremonies in the main city, the Aymara practiced a more localized religion in their various towns. For example, each Aymara community had *chulpas*, or local ceremonial and burial houses, in which to hold rituals without having to travel to a central city location.

The Aymara were extremely organized and consisted of at least seven different major "nations" of Aymara-speaking peoples. Each nation was divided into two separate kingdoms, each governed by its own king. Thus, the two largest nations, the Lupaca (southwest of Lake Titicaca) and the Colla (near present-day Puno, Peru), each had two governments to accommodate their two kingdoms. Each kingdom controlled different territories. However, the Lupaca and the Colla warred with one another constantly until around 1430, when the Lupaca finally conquered the Colla.

Kin groupings, or *ayllus*, were a vital part of Aymara society. The ayllus were the community landowners who worked the fields collectively. Though all Aymara Indians desired *ayllu* membership, the settlements also had regional chiefs called *kurakas*. These rulers held land independently of the ayllus and could demand free labor of the ayllu members they governed.

The Aymara cultivated potatoes and cereal crops and were able to increase their food supply through irrigation and the process of freeze-drying crops. They herded llamas and alpacas as pack animals and for their meat, milk, and wool. In fact, camelids were so fundamental to the Aymaran way of life that the wealth of the kingdoms was measured by the number of llamas and alpacas they owned.

Like the Tiahuanaco before them, the Aymara valued trade with other groups in the eastern valleys and along the Pacific Coast. In exchange for Altiplano meats, potatoes, quinoa, and wool products, the coastal inhabitants paid with fish and salt, and the people of the subtropical valleys with corn, coca, fruit, and vegetables.

Since the Aymara were both warlike and wealthy, they became the dominant peoples of most of Bolivia, as well as of a section of southern Peru, by the late fourteenth century. They completely dominated the Uru, another major ethnic group in the southern Andes at the time. The Uru had preceded the Aymara in the region, but by the twelfth century, the Aymara had reduced the group to poor fishermen and landless workers.

As population and prosperity continued to grow throughout the Andes, the Aymara found themselves in direct competition with the Quechua-speaking nation in the region of Cuzco, Peru, north of Lake Titicaca. Little did they know that by the late fifteenth century the Cuzco-Quechua speakers, later to be known as the Incas, would emerge as the most powerful of the new Andean nations.

THE MIGHTY INCA EMPIRE (1450–1530 A.D.)

As the rise of Inca power also marked the rise of Quechua culture over that of the Aymara, no one really knows whether the Incas were Quechuas or if they even originally spoke Quechua. It is known that Quechua became the universal language of the empire, and this helped to unify the people and lands that the Incas conquered. When the Incas subdued a group of people, they transplanted peaceful populations already assimilated, or integrated, into the culture and imperial framework to the newly conquered areas. In this way, the Quechua language was introduced into lands lying even on the frontiers of the empire. Today, Quechuas, who were likely settled there under Inca rule, populate the southern and eastern parts of the Bolivian Altiplano.

Even as conquered areas fell under Inca rule, the Inca rulers seemed to respect the cultures and languages of the defeated peoples, imposing only their religion. For example, in the Lake Titicaca region, the Aymaran culture and language remained practically intact (and still is today). There is also evidence that the Incas did not fully conquer the territory known as highland Bolivia until approximately 60 years before the Spanish conquest. According to local tradition, this assimilation was not easily accomplished; the Aymara fought bitterly against the Inca armies.

The roots of the Inca dynasty are shrouded in mythology. Some legends actually locate the origin of the Inca Empire in what is now Bolivia. One common myth explains that Manco Kapac, the earliest Inca noble, and Mama Ocllo, his sister, rose out of Lake Titicaca on the Isla del Sol. The two attempted to instruct the people of the Altiplano in the arts of civilization, but failed. Only then did they start the journey that led them to Cuzco, the Incan capital city (the city's name means "navel of the world").

Incan society was extremely well organized and strictly hierarchical. Each male person was assigned an appointed place in society based on the circumstances of his birth. Though the common man remained an agriculturalist or herdsman, the Inca state was actually a humane ruling entity based on equality and justice. Each *ayllu*, or group of families, had its own land to cultivate communally, but everyone also was expected to work the state-owned lands belonging to the Inca, or king. In this way, the state was able to collect taxes in the form of surplus crops to maintain the empire. These "taxes" were sent to local, regional, and national storehouses to feed the Inca and his family, the privileged classes, the nobles, the religious orders, and the government officials. A share of the crops was stored as reserves for such emergencies as famine or war. If harvests were poor in any section of the nation, surplus was distributed from these stores to prevent starvation of the *ayllu* affected. Even though the Indian peasants worked hard for the Inca, they also knew that the state would take care of them should they ever need help.

Although taxation was in the form of goods rather than money, it was nevertheless strict and recorded using a device called a *quipu*. A quipu consisted of a string from which hung secondary strings. The position of knots on the secondary string indicated places in the decimal system, and the number of knots represented the number of units at those places. The Incas were able to maintain detailed records of domestic animals, human population, crop yields, and even farmland with the system. The Incas never did develop a written language, perhaps because the quipu was sufficient for their needs. Amazingly, the quipu method is so efficient that some estate owners in Bolivia continued to use it for record keeping well into the twentieth century.

By the time the Spanish conquered Bolivia in the sixteenth century, the Incan territory covered a major part of the western half of the South American continent. To be exact, their lands spread from north of the equator to central Chile over an area of 380,000 square miles (984,200 square kilometers) and a linear distance of 3,000 miles (4,828 kilometers). How was the Incan state able to govern over such a vast area? The answer is a network of intricately placed all-weather roads, served by *tambos,* or combination roadhouses and storehouses. Relay runners, or *chasquis,* carried mail and crops, and other items from one tambo to another. They created an astonishing communications network that kept the government in contact with all areas of the far-flung empire. The chasquis were so efficient that often they could relay messages faster than it takes an airmail letter to cover the same distance today!

The Incas left an undeniable mark on Bolivia through their extensive road system, architecture, metal and ceramics artifacts, and the Quechua language. Their empire was marked by its powerful reign and by the highly sophisticated nature of its government and economic structure. Amazingly enough, despite all these advances, the duration of Inca rule in Bolivia was only 80 years.

The woodcut illustration shows the Spanish conqueror Francisco Pizarro (c. 1475–1541) meeting the incumbent Incan emperor Atahuallpa, in approximately 1533 A.D.

4

The Spanish Conquest

T he amazing story of the Inca civilization ended with the arrival of Spaniards in Peru in 1532. Within one year of landing on the Peruvian coast, Francisco Pizarro and Diego de Almagro and their conquistadors pushed their way toward the Incan capital at Cuzco in search of riches and land. At the time, Atahuallpa ruled the Inca Empire. Unlike earlier emperors, he was not considered the true descendent of the Sun God, the Incas' most revered deity.

FALL OF THE INCAS

When the Spanish arrived, the Incas initially trusted them. They treated the bearded white men with respect, believing them to be gods sent by a previous emperor, Viracocha Inca. They believed the Spaniards had been sent as revenge for Atahuallpa's violation of custom, in which he, in fear, had had the true heir of the Sun God murdered. Atahuallpa's actions had therefore not only ended the bloodline of the royal Inca family, but also shamed the entire dynasty and broke the power of the hierarchy.

The Spanish conquistadors took advantage of the weaknesses created by Atahuallpa and the initial trust given them by the Incas. By 1535, the Inca capital city of Cuzco had fallen, and lands had been divided between the two leaders of the Spanish forces. Armies were quickly dispatched to the Lake Titicaca region in the belief that gold and other mineral wealth there would be one of the most promising conquests.

The Spanish used religion to justify their acts of conquest. They relied on messages and miracles supposedly sent by the Holy Virgin and spread word to the Indians of a new god. The Indians so feared what they believed to be the Spaniards' supernatural powers that they relented to them without difficulty or resistance. In 1542, the Spanish annexed present-day Bolivia. The claim included what was called the Audencia of Charcas of the Viceroyalty of Peru, also known as Alto (high) Peru.

During the Spanish occupation, Bolivian towns grew rapidly. The town of La Plata, now Sucre, was founded in 1538. It became the Spanish capital of Charcas in 1559 and is still Bolivia's official (constitutional, not administrative) capital city today. La Paz was founded in 1548 as a Spanish administrative center.

In the beginning, the Spanish left many of the customs and social structures in place in their newly conquered lands. They imposed a system of required labor similar to the Inca system of the past. Eventually, however, Spanish rule became more forceful and driven by greed. Much of the economy became based on the extraction of mineral resources and export of this wealth to Spain. Colonial society centered on the *hacienda*, or large estate, where aristocratic landowners could rule the indigenous people. Indians became tenant farmers, practically owned by the Spanish lords. They were given small subsistence-sized plots of land in exchange for supplying their conquerors with food and labor.

MINES AT POTOSÍ

The Bolivian mining community of Potosí is the world's highest city, located at an elevation of 13,048 feet (3,977 meters). But this fact is not its most important legacy. Instead, Potosí, and more specifically its *Cerro Rico* (Rich Mountain), is the site of a silver mine that produced great wealth for Spain. The wealth came with a high price, however, as thousands of enslaved Indians lost their lives working under harsh conditions there.

According to legend, in 1462, an Incan king, Huayna Capac, had almost begun excavation at Potosí. He was halted by a mysterious voice which commanded that he not remove any silver from the hill because it was destined for other owners. The Inca then named the hill *Ppotojsi*, a Quechua word meaning "ruin" or "spoil." Then, supposedly in 1544, a wandering Indian man named Diego Huallpa climbed Sumaj Orcko, as Cerro Rico was then called, searching for some lost llamas. Into the evening, he became tired and cold and built a fire to keep warm. By the morning, the fire had smelted a vein of silver. Huallpa included his friend, Guanca, in his secret, and they began to mine for the silver treasure. Sadly, Guanca told the Spanish of his fortune, and they quickly claimed the mountain as their own, founding the city of Potosí in 1545.

When commercial exploitation of Cerro Rico began, people flocked to the site in search of riches. Eighteen months after the Spanish learned of the silver at Potosí, the population had climbed to 14,000. And within 25 years, the city's population had exploded to more than 120,000. By 1650, 160,000 people lived in Potosí, making it the largest city in all of Latin America, a position it held for some decades. For years, the mine at Potosí was the world's most productive. The silver extracted from it bankrolled practically the entire Spanish economy, especially the monarchy, for two centuries.

Most of the labor used in the mines, textile mills, and on the haciendas was extracted from Aymara Indians of the Altiplano, or Quechua Indians of the temperate valleys. Taxes levied by the Spanish Crown on Bolivian communities were so high that they could be met only by sending workers into the mines. It is estimated that this system of forced labor, or *mita*, involved an average of 14 to 15 percent of the inhabitants of any given highland community at any one time. Often mines were so distant from workers' communities that by the time a laborer returned to his home, he had to leave again to serve his next term.

Brutal working conditions ensured a short life span for many of the miners. Those who didn't die from exhaustion or accidents usually succumbed to pulmonary pneumonia within a few years. The Spanish also imported millions of African slaves to increase the labor force. In 1572, the Viceroy Toledo enacted a law requiring all Indian slaves over the age of 18 to work in shifts of 12 hours. Each worker would remain in the mines working, sleeping, and eating underground for four months at a time without seeing the light of day. When they finally emerged, workers' eyes were covered to prevent damage from the sunlight. It is estimated that, between 1545 and 1825, several million Indians and Africans died from the horrible conditions in the mines at Potosí.

The Africans, who were feared by the Indians, were unaccustomed to strenuous work at such high elevations. Many of them, therefore, were eventually used for domestic work in the town of Potosí. The Africans who were able to survive migrated to the warmer climate of the Yungas. They became an Aymara-speaking minority in the region and colonized areas mainly for the production of coca. Chewing coca leaves had been the exclusive right of the Incan elite, but the Spanish introduced the leaves to Indian workers to keep them working without complaint. Many, if not most, of the miners at Potosí chewed coca leaves. It helped them face the hardships of mining by numbing their senses to the cold and suppressing their appetites.

The Spaniards considered Indians to be inferior and therefore sought to destroy the entire indigenous culture. They even required that the Indians wear Spanish-style clothing. Popular belief holds that the distinctive hats and *polleras*, or multilayered skirts, worn in Bolivia today originated with mandates from the Spanish monarchy. The mortality rate among indigenous people increased during this time, not only from the horrendous working conditions in the mines, but also from European diseases against which the Indians had no resistance. By the mid-seventeenth century, 100 years after the Spanish arrival in South America, the indigenous population of Bolivia had been halved.

Potosí's official coat of arms still reads "*Soy el rico Potosí, del mundo soy el tesoro; soy el rey de los montes, envidia soy de los reyes*" (I am rich Potosí, the treasure of the world; the king of mountains, the envy of kings). The Spanish referred to Potosí as the "Imperial City," because no other city in the world could match its wealth during the sixteenth and seventeenth centuries. The city's influence was far-reaching, both in the way it affected the indigenous people and how it fed the coffers of Spain's monarchy. During the eighteenth century, Potosí's rich silver veins became exhausted, and Bolivia, or Alto Peru, lost much of its power.

JESUIT MISSIONS

While enormous wealth was being sought in Potosí, souls were being saved in the eastern lowlands of Bolivia. Spanish conquistadors had little trouble conquering the Indians of highland Bolivia, but the native peoples of the eastern lowlands were much more challenging. Only the Jesuits, a Roman Catholic religious order of priests, succeeded in settling the remote tropical villages and winning converts to Christianity. Today, six Jesuit Mission churches survive in the region surrounding Santa Cruz.

After the Jesuits arrived in Lima, Peru, in 1569, they first introduced Christianity to the Aymara people around Lake Titicaca. Soon they made their way to Paraguay to form an autonomous religious state. From there, they ventured northward into territory unexplored by Europeans, the eastern lowland areas of Bolivia. Their main goal was to convert the local, historically nomadic, indigenous communities to Christianity. They also persuaded the Indians to live in communal settlements. These self-sufficient communes were called *reducciones* and normally contained between 2,000 and 4,000 inhabitants. The people of the communities were divided into productive units, headed by two or three Jesuit priests. The communities and their churches were well planned. Naturally, a large elaborate church was constructed in each settlement with labor provided by Indians under the supervision of priests.

Priests also encouraged the Indians to form military units. They sought to defend the settlements against attacks from the Portuguese in Brazil, the Spanish in the west, and more aggressive native tribes. For a while, these armies were the most powerful and well trained in all of South America.

The Jesuit experiment brought economic benefits to the sparsely populated tropics of Bolivia. Priests introduced animal husbandry and agricultural practices to the nomadic hunters and gatherers. In exchange, Indians taught the priests how to survive in the tropical environment. As a result of this collaboration, the missions grew and eventually formed a commercial trade network with the Aymara and Quechua peoples of the highlands. They traded textiles, cotton, honey, beeswax, and native artwork in exchange for raw silver from the mines and other goods.

Because the Jesuits were mainly concerned with saving the native people's souls, many of the beliefs and customs held sacred by the Indians were suppressed. In fact, the Jesuits were so successful in instilling the new religion that little is known today about the indigenous cultures prior to their arrival.

Converting Indians to Christianity was not the priests' only goal. They also worked to promote cultural and educational development among the Indians. They succeeded in fostering art within the communities. Many locals became true artisans, trained in woodworking, making jewelry from precious metals, and creating textiles. They taught them to craft and play instruments, such as harps and violins. Some of the local instruments were superior to those found in Europe at the time. Each community had an organized orchestra that performed concerts and Italian operas. Orchestral music may have captivated the Indians, thereby playing a role in developing their interest in Jesuit ideas, but perhaps more influential to the Indians was the promise by the priests that whoever chose to participate in the activities of the *reducciones* would be exempt from laboring in the mines of Potosí.

Even though Bolivian Jesuit communities functioned successfully for many years, 1767 saw the expulsion of the Jesuits and the abandonment of the missions. The Spanish Crown likely regarded their influence and success in the tropics as a threat to the power of Spain. King Carlos III signed the Order of Expulsion, which evicted the Jesuits from the continent. However, other priests arrived soon after the Jesuits departed. These priests treated the Indians poorly, fostering hatred among the native tribes while prospering from the livestock and crops introduced by the Jesuits. All that remains today of the Jesuit experiment are six beautiful churches.

FIGHT FOR INDEPENDENCE

The struggle for Bolivia's independence was really a conflict between one elite group and another. Throughout the colonial period, people born in Spain, or *peninsulares*, held most of the power. Those people of pure Spanish ancestry born in Bolivia,

Portrait of Simón Bolívar, a Venezuelan who was nicknamed "The Liberator." The *República de Bolívar* was named for him in 1825; the name was later changed to Bolivia.

or *criollos*, had been constantly excluded from administrative and religious jobs. The criollos became increasingly frustrated with high taxes and trade restrictions that only benefited Spain.

While Spain was busy defending its own borders against Napoleon's armies, faculty and others at the University of San

Francisco Xavier in Sucre (then known as Chuquisaca) called for independence of all of Spain's American colonies. The date was May 25, 1809.

Spain attempted to restore its rule over the next few years, but with the leadership of a Venezuelan named Simón Bolívar, the criollo elites were able to rise up against Spanish authority. On December 9, 1824, Bolívar's general, Antonio José de Sucre, defeated the Spanish at the battle of Ayacucho in Peru. This event helped Peru gain its independence. From there, General Sucre entered Alto Peru and defeated the Spanish at the battle of Tumusla on April 2, 1825. Spanish colonial rule in Bolivia seemed to be over.

Bolivia was declared independent of Spain on August 6, 1825. In honor of Simón Bolívar, the great liberator, the country was named República de Bolívar, later changed to Bolivia. Simón Bolívar and Antonio José de Sucre became Bolivia's first and second presidents.

The Bolivian city of Potosi and more precisely, its *Cerro Rico*, or Rich Mountain, is the site of a famous silver mine in Bolivia. The riches from the mine financed the Spanish Empire for two centuries. Today, a project has been launched to exploit what is left of the world's richest silver deposits at Potosi.

5

Post-Independence and Modern Bolivia

The new republic of Bolivia faced many problems following its independence from Spain. Huge military expenditures in the wars over independence had exhausted the economy. Bolivia suffered from many difficulties, including continuing political instability and problems securing its borders against incursions by neighbors. The mining industry was in sharp decline because of inadequate investment capital and scarcity of labor. During this period, many mines were abandoned, flooded, or otherwise destroyed.

Furthermore, Bolivia's agricultural production was low. The country was forced to import food—even staples normally grown in the rural areas—to support the Indian population. After independence, most of the land ownership changed hands from the Spanish to the criollo elite. At the end of the nineteenth century, wealthy landowners ended the Indian system of communal lands. Many of these lands were added to their already huge ranches, called *latifundios*. The Indians, who had suffered terribly under the mita, or compulsory labor imposed by the Spanish, became serfs, required to work and live on the latifundios. The fruits of their labor were therefore taken by the criollo elite instead of used to feed themselves.

LOSS OF TERRITORY

Bolivia's war for independence would be the last conflict from which the country would emerge victorious. At the time of independence in 1825, Bolivia encompassed over 772,204 square miles (2 million square kilometers). By 1935, just 100 years after independence, only half the original territory remained. The country had lost half of its territory to wars and disputes with its neighbors.

The first and most considerable loss came in the 1879–1884 War of the Pacific against Chile. As a result of this conflict, Chile gained 528 miles (850 kilometers) of coastline from Bolivia and Peru. Bolivia was devastated by the loss. It had lost its window on the Pacific Ocean, including its seaport at Antofagasta. It also lost vast deposits of copper and the nitrate-rich sands of the Atacama Desert. Chile attempted to compensate Bolivia for the loss by allowing a railroad from La Paz to the coast and granting free port privileges at Antofagasta. However, in the minds of many Bolivians, these measures could never make up for losing the precious seacoast, and resentment towards Chile still exists today.

In the following years, Peru and Argentina each robbed Bolivia of small amounts of territory, but the next major loss was to Brazil in 1903. During the rubber boom, Brazil succeeded in annexing Bolivia's remote Acre territory, an area that stretches from Bolivia's present Amazonian borders to halfway along Peru's eastern border. The area was home to vast stands of wild rubber trees. Because of the potential natural wealth, Brazil issued a dispute over the area and sent in its army. Brazil convinced the people of Acre to secede from Bolivia and promptly took possession of the territory. Brazil also attempted to compensate Bolivia for the loss by building a railroad. This rail line was intended to open up the remote northern areas of Bolivia and to provide an outlet to the Amazon Basin. The railway was never completed.

The third major loss of Bolivian territory occurred during the Chaco War from 1932–1935. The Chaco War involved a border dispute between Bolivia and Paraguay. For more than a decade, the United States' Standard Oil Company had been drilling for oil on the Chaco plain. The company believed that this and other areas in the region held rich petroleum deposits. That the frontier between the two countries had never been truly defined only compounded the problem. An all-out war began. During the war, Standard Oil supported Bolivia, while another major U.S. oil company, Shell Oil, sided with Paraguay. Paraguayan troops were much more familiar with the terrain and the hot and humid climate than were the Bolivian soldiers, most of whom were from the Bolivian highlands. It is little wonder that many Bolivian war veterans believed that insects, climate, and disease had been their greatest adversaries! By 1935, Bolivia had lost the war, as well as 55,000 of its soldiers. The additional sought-after oil reserves were never found, but Bolivia retained a small section of the Chaco where oil had already been located. Today, those fields allow Bolivia to remain self-sufficient in oil production.

THE RISE OF TIN

Silver was the most important mineral during the colonial era, but tin began to grow in significance during the late nineteenth century. Historically, limited tin mining had occurred in the Potosí area, but Bolivia lacked the transportation facilities needed to export large quantities of it to European markets. In the 1890s, the railway was extended to Oruro, and tin mining became more profitable. At the same time, European tin production was declining, and the United States needed more tin, especially during wartime. The result was a Bolivian tin boom after 1900. With the development of tin mining operations in Oruro and the northern part of the Potosí Department, La Paz soon became the financial and service center of the entire mining industry.

Many men became rich from the tin mines, but three in particular controlled most of the industry: Simón Patiño, Carlos Aramayo, and Mauricio Hochschild. Because the government depended on taxes and fees from tin production to expand federal reserves, these tin magnates wielded substantial influence over government policy. The tin barons employed lawyers and politicians to represent their interests in government affairs.

The tin boom also affected Bolivia's human geography. Most of the labor was provided by Indian peasants who began to move out of the countryside and into the larger mining towns to find work. However, the working conditions had hardly improved since colonial times. The demand for workers' rights led to the creation of a union in 1912, the First National Congress of Workers.

In the late 1920s, however, the bottom fell out from under the mining industry. This event would help lead to another period of economic and political turbulence, and eventually to revolution.

POLITICAL INSTABILITY AND REVOLUTION

Historically, Bolivia's political situation has been turbulent. Between 1825 and 1982, the country experienced more than 188 *coup d'états*, or attempts to overthrow the government. In 1836, the longest lasting Bolivian government of the nineteenth century, that of Andrés Santa Cruz (1829 to 1839), was overthrown by Chile and Argentina when he attempted to unite Bolivia with Peru. In 1899, business groups from La Paz and the tin-mining areas led a rebellion that resulted in the central-ization of government in La Paz, though Sucre remains the titular capital.

In the 1940s, a new nationalist political party was formed by a few young intellectuals and called the Movimiento Nacionalista Revolucionario (MNR), or National Revolution Movement. MNR claimed to stand for the liberation of Bolivia's poor peasants and was successful in uniting the masses to fight for popular reform. The party's representatives were able to incite labor unrest on the part of Indian tin miners against their absentee bosses. By airing their grievances over the horrendous working conditions, low pay, and export of profits to Europe, the miners helped increase the political awareness of all Bolivian workers.

In the 1951 presidential elections, Victor Paz Estenssoro, the MNR candidate, was victorious. The incumbent govern-ment, however, staged a military coup and refused to relinquish its power. The coup provoked an armed uprising by the miners of the country; the revolt was known as the April Revolution of 1952. The miners, supported by groups of police, peasants, urban factory workers, and members of the lower-middle class, bravely fought the incumbents' military junta and won. With this victory, President Paz Estenssoro was able to nationalize the mines, expel the tin barons and their massive economic and political influence, and set up a state entity in charge of mining interests, called COMIBOL (Corporación Minera de Bolivia).

President Paz Estenssoro also began the Agrarian Reform Program of 1953, which ended the feudal agricultural system and redistributed lands of the latifundios to the peasant farmers. Finally, it seemed the poor people of Bolivia would be able to control their own destinies. However, from the 1960s through the mid-1980s, the Bolivian political scene was dominated by coups and military governments. The governments of this time were often very different from

Victor Paz Estenssoro served a total of four terms as president and was known for leading the country's April Revolution of 1952. With this victory he nationalized the mines. He also promoted land reforms to redistribute land to the peasant farmers.

one another. Some of these dictatorships were oppressive, seeking to subdue political opponents, labor union activists, and miners. Some used violence to repress the people. Others were more liberal, hoping to give even more rights to the peasantry.

ERNESTO "CHÉ" GUEVARA

Among the many revolutionaries who attempted to overthrow the Bolivian government during this time was Ernesto "Ché" Guevara. Guevara, an Argentinean by birth, was a member of the Communist Party and believed in an equal society for all people. He worked with Fidel Castro in Cuba in the late 1950s, and even tried to spread his socialist messages as far as Africa.

In 1966, Guevara and a band of guerrillas stationed themselves 155 miles (250 kilometers) southwest of Santa Cruz, Bolivia, hoping to create a revolution among the rural subsistence farmers of the countryside. Most of these *campesinos* wanted nothing to do with Guevara's talk of social rebellion, and his attempts were usually either ignored or met with suspicion. Ché Guevara was finally captured on October 8, 1967, by United States military forces trained by the U.S. Central Intelligence Agency (CIA). He was executed by the Bolivian army and buried in an undisclosed grave near the town of Vallegrande.

The revolutionary spirit is still alive in the Bolivian people, however. Practically every town has a monument to the liberator, Simón Bolívar, and Ché Guevara still lives on T-shirts and in graffiti. It is in this spirit that Bolivians have demonstrated against their government in the last few years of the twentieth century over issues such as economic inflation, coca growing, and privatization of utilities. These issues continue to affect the country and will likely prove difficult challenges for the government in the years to come.

La Paz is the capital city of Bolivia. It is backed by the magnificent snow-capped peaks of the Cordillera Real, the highest peak of which is Illimani at 21,184 feet (6,458 meters) above sea level.

6

People and Culture

B olivia is the fifth largest of the 13 South American countries in size and the eighth largest in population, with 8.4 million people. The country is the about the same size as France and Spain combined but contains only 8.4 percent as many people. Bolivia's population density is only 21 people per square mile (as compared to France's 284 per square mile and Spain's 205 per square mile). There are many reasons for this low density of people, not the least of which are the country's diverse and difficult environmental conditions. Much of southern and western Bolivia consists of areas of high elevations and dry climate, whereas the northeast is remote, wet, and forested. Physical geography definitely plays an important role influencing where the Bolivian people live.

Low population density also can be attributed to relatively high infant mortality rates and low life expectancies. Bolivia's infant mortality rate stands at 57.5 deaths per 1,000 live births per year. Life expectancies are 62 years for males and 67 years for females. Both of these figures are comparable to the average longevity for less-developed countries. The population is growing at an annual rate of 2.3 percent, a full percentage point above the world average 1.3. Bolivia's population is both young and growing at a rate greater than the country's economic growth.

WHERE PEOPLE LIVE

Strangely enough, despite its bitterly cold and dry climate, the Altiplano is home to more than half of Bolivia's population. This settlement pattern has held since pre-Spanish times. Most settlement (where people live) is concentrated in the northern end of the Altiplano, in La Paz and Oruro, and around Lake Titicaca. The Altiplano around Lake Titicaca has a relatively mild climate and favorable growing conditions that help to support a high population density. Southward on the Altiplano, settlement tends to thin rapidly because of aridity. Communities do exist wherever adequate water is found, as along the Desaguadero River. Small settled valleys can be found through-out this area, but much of the arid plateau supports only a few seminomadic shepherds. Rural settlement on the Altiplano is in sharp decline as well, as people migrate in increasing numbers to the larger cities and towns.

Because of the improved economic opportunities in these urban areas, population is growing in the valleys, with most people living in or around the crowded cities of Cochabamba, Sucre, or Tarija. The tropical Yungas region, on the other hand, remains only moderately settled because of steep terrain that prevents easy access.

Over the last 50 years, valley settlement has been directly linked to increased government support for colonization of these areas. In-migration began with the Agrarian Reform after the 1952 National Revolution. To boost agricultural productivity and reduce population pressure on the densely populated Altiplano, the government encouraged peasant farmers to relocate to the lower-lying areas. The strong success of the government's colonization plan has also caused problems. Bolivia's valleys are now experiencing considerable strain on land and infrastructure, such as water, electricity, and transportation routes. Some of the immigrants from the higher elevations are able to only barely make a living from the production of coffee, coca, rice, and citrus fruits. Others live in rural poverty, unable to acquire land to farm.

Most of the valleys' recent population growth has been concentrated at the middle elevations and near access roads that provide a link to markets. Today, approximately 30 percent of Bolivia's population now lives in the Yungas and other valleys.

Population and settlement also are increasing rapidly in the eastern lowlands, now home to about 20 percent of the Bolivian population. Since 1952, the government has centralized capital investment in the Santa Cruz Department. As a result, much of the region is dedicated to large-scale agriculture as well as natural gas and timber extraction. The eastern lowlands are Bolivia's most important economic area. Consequently, people are flocking to the Santa Cruz Department in search of economic opportunity, and Santa Cruz is Bolivia's fastest-growing city. In 1950, its population was well under 100,000; today its metropolitan area has swelled to nearly one million.

Other than the concentration in the city of Santa Cruz, most of the lowland region's population is widely scattered. Large commercial farms producing sugarcane, cotton, or rice are in areas with easy access to Santa Cruz. In other areas, ranches, towns, and settlements are clustered near riverbanks to facilitate transportation where major roads have not yet been developed. Most of the heavily forested, tropical, northern half of the lowlands region is sparsely settled. Only small and widely scattered Indian settlements break an otherwise largely undeveloped landscape.

DOMESTIC AND INTERNATIONAL MIGRATION

As is happening throughout much of the world, Bolivia is losing its rural population as people migrate to more urban areas. In particular, young people aged 18 to 25 are leaving their rural communities in search of better opportunities and living conditions in the larger towns and cities. Urban centers offer excitement, amenities, better education and health care, and greater potential for employment. While some return to their rural roots, most find the fast-paced lifestyle of La Paz, Cochabamba, or Santa Cruz exciting and difficult to leave. Thus Bolivia's transition from a rural-to-urban society has been quite sharp. In 1976, only 42 percent of Bolivians lived in towns; by 1992, 57 percent resided in urban areas; a decade later, in 2002, the urban population had risen to 64 percent. The trend shows no sign of abating.

The country's departments themselves show marked differences in patterns of population growth and decline. For example, the Department of Santa Cruz has grown twice as fast as the national average in recent decades. The Altiplano, although still Bolivia's most heavily populated region, has been rapidly losing people since tin mining declined.

Besides the internal migrations occurring in Bolivia, the country also is experiencing an increase in international out-migration. The country's economic situation has been so bleak in recent years that people are leaving. Most emigrants (people who leave) go to Argentina, the United States, or Europe, particularly Spain, where they can speak Spanish. These people are normally in search of an education or better jobs enabling them to send money home to their families in Bolivia. Occasionally a parent may be gone from his or her children for years, working in some foreign land and sending money back to help support many relatives at home. This type of migration is causing a "brain drain," as the better-educated people decide to leave Bolivia for opportunities abroad.

PEOPLE AND LANGUAGE

Bolivia contains a wealth of cultural diversity. Most of its people can be divided into three main groups: about 50 to 60 percent are of pure indigenous blood (Native Americans); about one-third are *mestizos,* or people of mixed European and indigenous ancestry; and the remainder are of European origin. Approximately 1 percent of the population is of African heritage, descendents of slaves who worked in the mines at Potosí.

Population composition varies from place to place. The Lake Titicaca region is almost purely indigenous as is more than half the population of La Paz. On the other hand, about 75 percent of the people in Cochabamba, the Yungas, and Santa Cruz are either mestizo or European. Tarija, a city near the border with Argentina, is the most European of all of Bolivia's cities.

Most of the highland indigenous population is either Quechua or Aymara. This population is very traditional, and many indigenous people resist cultural change. The Indians north of the Altiplano normally speak Aymara and number approximately two million. Those living in other mountain areas or in the valleys mainly speak Quechua, the language of the Incas. They number about three million. Today, the two groups remain distinct in language and culture.

In the more rural areas, many Native Americans, especially women, speak no Spanish whatsoever. It is common for some men in a village to understand and speak some Spanish, although their native tongue is used exclusively for day-to-day conversation. An increasing number of young people also are learning English. About 70 percent of Bolivians speak Quechua, Aymara, or Tupi-Guaraní (the dominant Indian language in the Bolivian lowlands). Quechua and Aymara are both official national languages, along with Spanish, but were not taught in the public schools until recently. Today, the government is placing more emphasis on Bolivia's native languages, so that future generations will know the tongues used by their ancestors.

The Aymara

The Aymara are descendents of the great culture at Tiahuanaco, and for the most part they still reside in the Lake Titicaca region. They are a strong ethnic group, whose people have adapted both culturally and physically to the region's harsh climate and high elevation. Here, well-developed hearts and lungs, resulting in unusually large chests, allow residents to efficiently use the thin air of the Altiplano.

Aymara are a fiercely proud people and may seem cold to outsiders. Although the Aymara campesinos (or rural people) have owned their land since the Agrarian Reform of 1952, they are still unimaginably poor. On average, a family on the Altiplano lives on approximately US $11.50 a month in wages, mostly from meager crop sales. Their life expectancy of 46 years is lower than the national average and one of the lowest in the world. Infant mortality, with 72 deaths per 1,000 live births, is tragically high and in the Western Hemisphere is exceeded only by that of Haiti. Rural life can be very difficult on the high plains of the Altiplano.

The Quechua

The Quechua people are more varied geographically than the Aymara. Quechuas live in the fertile valleys of Cochabamba, on the high plateaus of Potosí, throughout the Chuquisaca Department, and in parts of the Oruro Department. Some Quechua communities remain isolated, but many have been influenced by the outside world. Numerous Quechua also have migrated to urban areas.

As mentioned earlier, indigenous people living in urban

The Aymara peoples are descendants of the great ethnic line at Tiahuanaco and many still live in the Lake Titicaca region. These Aymara children are posing with their llamas.

areas who continue to wear traditional dress are called *cholos* (or *cholas* if referring to an entirely female group). Many of the cholos living in Cochabamba are native Quechuas who also speak Spanish. They have abandoned their traditional way of life for a life in the city. Campesino Quechuas consider cholos more Western in their manners, which tends to weaken their ethnic uniqueness. The cholo lifestyle has influenced many parts of Quechua culture, including dance and music.

Mestizos

Mestizos form the most widely distributed ethnic group in Bolivia. Originally, people in this category were defined on the basis of mixed European and native Indian ancestry. In Bolivia, however, language, urban orientation, livelihood, manners, and style of dress often define a person of mestizo heritage. Most people of mestizo descent in Bolivia speak Spanish instead of an indigenous language and they live in cities or suburban areas. They are often more established economically than the indigenous Aymara or Quechua, and they wear Western-style clothing instead of traditional dress.

Bolivians of European Descent

The Bolivians of European ancestry are not as widely distributed geographically as are mestizos. They are found mainly in cities or in the rapidly developing Santa Cruz Department. Some are direct descendents of the early Spanish conquerors, but there are also communities of German-speaking Mennonites, descendents of Jewish refugees from Nazi Europe, and Eastern European refugees. Others include small numbers of scientific researchers, aid workers, and missionaries. There are also small clusters of Middle Eastern and Asian people, consisting mostly of Chinese, Japanese, Palestinians, and Punjabis. For the most part, these immigrants speak Spanish or their own native tongues.

Other Ethnic Groups

The lowland areas of Bolivia contain roughly 150,000 indigenous people. They are different in dress, language, customs, and physical features than the upland Quechua and Aymara. These people are divided into some 30 groups, or tribes. They include the Guaraní (numbering about 20,000), the Chiquitano (about 15,000), the Guaravo (about 15,000), and the smaller Ayoreo, Chiriguano, Chimane, and Mojo groups. Though the Jesuits settled many of their lowland communities into missions over 300 years ago, each tribe speaks its own language. Only recently have many of these isolated groups assimilated into Bolivian culture.

Afro-Bolivians number about 17,000 and live mostly in the Yungas region near La Paz. Most speak Spanish, but a few continue to speak Aymara. Often they wear the traditional dress of the highland Quechua or Aymara Indians.

RELIGION

Over 95 percent of Bolivia's population is Roman Catholic. In reality, however, the religion is a mix of Christian ideals with a blend of animistic doctrines, rites, and superstitions. Animism is the worship of deities from the natural world, such as mountains, animals, or plants. The Catholic Church does not prohibit the mixing of Christianity and worship of the natural world amongst the country's Catholics. Therefore, a blend of Old and New World beliefs prevail in rural areas. Maintaining the indigenous traditions is fundamental to the culture of the Bolivian people and dates back before the Incan Empire.

In the 1980s, other Protestant religious groups began to gain increasing numbers of converts among Bolivia's urban and rural populations. Mormons, Jehovah's Witnesses, Seventh-Day Adventists, and members of Pentecostal faiths sent missionaries to the country during this time. Methodists, Mennonites, and

Over 95 percent of Bolivia's population is Roman Catholic, but their religion is a mix of Christian beliefs and worship of the natural world in the form of animals, plants, and mountains.

members of both the Bahai and Jewish faiths were also present. Many adherents to these denominations have faced discrimination, but although they remain a small minority, their numbers continue to grow.

The Aymara people are very religious. Though many Aymara call themselves Roman Catholics and do practice Christian rituals, they also continue to worship ancient animist spirits and perform ceremonies dating from the Tiahuanaco period.

Aymara believe that God, the supreme being, manifests himself/herself through the natural world in objects like the sun, the moon, the water, and the wind. To give thanks to God, they make offerings of *wilancha* (llama sacrifices) or *ch'alla* (sprinkling alcohol on the ground) to the *Pachamama* (the Mother Earth) and other spirits to protect the home and family. Aymara people also tend to be quite superstitious.

Aymara believe the high mountains are especially sacred. They perform rituals in the mountains that ask for a good harvest, enough water, and protection of families, or that just celebrate Pachamama. The *Yatiri*, a wise priest or priestess who serves as a community's spiritual leader usually leads these rituals. A Yatiri is able to "read" coca leaves to give community members spiritual guidance. Coca, therefore, is especially sacred to the Aymara.

Most Quechua also consider themselves Roman Catholic but practice a folk-type of religion similar to the Aymara, which includes worship of Pachamama. The Quechua people, however, seem to have fewer of the specialized religious rituals common to the Aymara.

These two women are supporters of the Socialism Movement Party candidate Evo Morales. They are standing outside the Parliament building in La Paz in August 2002. In the June election, Morales was found to run a close second to Gonzalo Sanchez de Lozada, but the election was, nonetheless, a victory for the indigenous people of Bolivia. Their strong showing brought the ethnic issue to the forefront of Bolivian politics.

Government

STRUCTURE OF GOVERNMENT

B olivia is a republic, similar to the United States, with legislative, executive, and judicial branches of government. The Congress and the president both reside in La Paz, the country's administrative capital, while the Supreme Court remains in Sucre, Bolivia's official titular capital city. Bolivia is divided politically into nine departments (similar to our states), which are subdivided into 112 provinces. The provinces are then subdivided into sections, and the sections into cantons.

The legislative branch of government consists of a Senate and a Chamber of Deputies. Three senators are elected for six-year terms in each of the nine departments. The Chamber of Deputies has 102 members who are also elected from the departments but who serve four-year terms.

In Bolivia, the president can serve for only one five-year term at a time. While a presidential candidate receiving a majority (more than 50 percent) of the popular vote would win the election, this rarely happens. If no candidate emerges with a majority vote, Congress selects the president from the top three candidates. Once in place, the president appoints a cabinet of 15 members, chooses prefects who head the country's departments, and selects other government officers for different localities. Because Congress is often forced to select the president (and indirectly his appointees), opponents believe that the democratic election process in Bolivia is unstable.

POLITICAL HISTORY

Bolivia's political history has indeed been unstable and marked by successive corrupt governments. Decisions made by past governments continue to affect the country economically and will likely have repercussions extending well into its future.

In 1952, the Nationalist Revolutionary Movement (MNR) party president, Victor Paz Estenssoro, helped lead the successful National Revolution. Through this win, he was able to carry out sweeping land reforms that returned agricultural land to the poor peasants, promoted rural education, and nationalized the largest tin mines. During these reforms, however, his government also committed many human rights abuses.

Between 1956 and 1960, Hernan Siles Zuazo served as president. Though the MNR party was beginning to disintegrate at this time, Victor Paz Estenssoro managed to become president again in 1960. Unfortunately, the government started to weaken and in 1964 was overthrown by a military junta. The junta established Rene Barrientos as president of the republic. The Barrientos regime, as it turned out, was no better for the country. It brutally persecuted political opponents and trade union activists and violently squashed any miners' rebellions. It appeared that the country had regressed to pre-revolution conditions. Barrientos's death in a mysterious air crash in

1969 was followed by a succession of weak governments as the country groped for strong political footing. Between 1969 and 1971, one coup followed another and a string of military dictators and juntas ruled the country. Some of the presidencies during this time lasted only weeks, or even days!

The military and the MNR, both alarmed by public disorder, installed General Hugo Banzer of the Acción Democrática Nacionalista (ADN) as president in 1971. On the positive side, the Banzer years were distinguished by relative political stability and unmatched economic growth. On the downside, however, his presidency was fraught with human rights abuses as he imprisoned or exiled thousands of Bolivians thought to be opponents to his government. All political parties except the Bolivian Socialist Falange (FSB) and MNR were banned, as were all labor unions. Banzer subjected the state universities to military supervision, and strict censorship existed throughout the country. Not surprisingly, he swiftly began to lose popularity. Banzer's dictatorship finally ended when President Jimmy Carter of the United States, dissatisfied with Bolivia's record on human rights violations, pressured the military government to hold general elections. Banzer lost the election in 1978 but refused to relinquish his position. He was finally overthrown that same year by another military government.

Elections were held in 1978, 1979, and 1980, but all were fraudulent and therefore inconclusive. Coups and counter-coups erupted during these years. Finally, General Luis Garcia Meza orchestrated a particularly ruthless and violent coup to secure the presidency. The years that followed saw unimpeded narcotics trafficking, more human rights abuses, and mishan-dling of money. Paramilitary groups descended on political opponents, capturing and torturing them. Garcia Meza's administration was the most corrupt Bolivia has ever known. Thankfully, it was finally brought to a close when a military rebellion forced him out of the presidency in 1981. Garcia Meza escaped to Brazil but was later convicted in Bolivia for various offenses, including murder. Brazil handed him over to Bolivian authorities, and he began serving a 30-year sentence for his brutal crimes in 1995.

After Garcia Meza was forced out of office, three other military governments controlled Bolivia over the next 14 months. Civil unrest drove the Congress to elect a new president, and in 1982, Hernan Siles Zuazo, who had already served as president from 1956 to 1960, was chosen. After a flailing period of economic mismanagement, weak leadership, and social pressure, Siles Zuazo called early elections and relinquished his presidency one year before the end of his term.

In Bolivia, if one candidate in a presidential election does not receive a majority of the votes, he may form a coalition, or alliance, with another candidate and pool his votes to create a majority. This happened in the 1985 elections when General Hugo Banzer won much of the popular vote but in the run-off lost to former president Victor Paz Estenssoro. Paz Estenssoro had formed a coalition with former vice president Jaime Paz Zamora and so was able to win a majority of the votes, subsequently being elected by Congress. When Paz Estenssoro took office for his fourth term, Bolivia was overcome by an astounding economic crisis following a few years of steady decline in exports.

The wild years in Bolivia continued into the late 1980s. Inflation was staggering, reaching an annual rate of 24,000 percent. There was rampant drug trafficking, civil unrest, and continuous strikes throughout the country. Somehow, however, President Paz Estenssoro was able to achieve stability, both economic and social, during his five-year term. He convinced the military to stay out of politics and almost completely ended the human rights violations that had plagued other administrations. Economics, however, suffered during this administration. Tin prices collapsed in October 1985, and 20,000 miners working for the mismanaged state mining company lost their jobs.

In the 1989 elections, Jaime Paz Zamora took the presidency after forming a coalition with Hugo Banzer. Paz Zamora was a moderate president, though his origins were rooted in communism. Fearing more inflation and even economic collapse, he continued to uphold his predecessor's economic reforms. Paz Zamora was tough on domestic terrorism, ordering attacks and crackdowns on some of the more active guerrilla armies. He was not so hard on drug trafficking, however, and even issued a decree in 1991 that gave lenient sentences to some of the country's biggest narcotics kingpins. His administration was also reluctant to support the U.S. plan for total eradication of the illegal coca used for cocaine production. His leniency was thought to stem from Paz Zamora's ties to major drug traffickers.

The 1993 elections continued to be fair and honest, with a peaceful democratic transition of power. The Congress elected the MNR's Gonzalo "Goni" Sanchez de Lozada president after he formed a coalition with two other parties. Sanchez de Lozada pursued aggressive economic and social reform. He began a controversial program, the capitalization program, which gave investors 50 percent ownership and management of public enterprises, such as the state oil company, electric utilities, and telecommunications system. Some people opposed his actions and created large and frequent public disturbances.

With help from a coalition with other parties, former dictator General Hugo Banzer again won the Bolivian presidential election in 1997 with 23 percent of the vote. In his first two years in office, Banzer, with support from the United States, called for an end to illegal coca cultivation and narcotics trafficking. By early 2000, Bolivia's economic situation worsened, especially in rural areas, and unemployment increased. Banzer, in failing health, left the office of president for the last time in 2001, and died shortly thereafter. Jorge Fernando Quiroga Ramirez finished out the remainder of Banzer's term, and in 2002 new elections took place.

THE 2002 ELECTIONS

The 2002 presidential elections in Bolivia took place on June 30, with a most surprising outcome. Evo Morales, the energetic leader of the coca growers' movement who had steadily been gaining a name for himself even before the campaign, came in second behind former president Gonzalo (Goni) Sanchez de Lozada. Sanchez de Lozada received 22 percent of the votes, while Morales received 21 percent. Although Goni, of the MNR party, eventually won the election with 84 votes in Congress to the 43 for Morales, it was definitely a victory of sorts for the indigenous population of Bolivia.

First, the victory of Morales's party, the Movimiento al Socialismo (MAS), or Socialism Movement Party, may affect the coca eradication efforts of the United States. Before the elections, the U.S. ambassador to Bolivia, Manuel Rocha, accused the coca growers of "narco-terrorism," and declared that the United States would stop giving aid to Bolivia if the people elected a president who "wants Bolivia to become a major cocaine exporter again." Needless to say, the United States' stance has not affected the loyalties of the peasant coca farmers, as Morales's percentage of the votes attests.

Second, part of Morales's platform included a return to national development and ownership for Bolivia. Morales believed that Bolivia should be responsible for its own natural resources. He wanted to establish control mechanisms to avoid selling valuable economic resources, such as minerals, water, oil, and gas, to private multinational companies. This means that President Gonzalo Sanchez de Lozada, himself a mine owner, must be very careful in continuing privatization of resources, as popular support for the practice appears to be dwindling.

Third, the success of MAS and one other indigenous party, Movimiento Indigenista Pachacuti (MIP), or Indigenous Pachacuti Movement, has brought the ethnic issue into the forefront of politics. Two-thirds of Bolivia's eight million people are indigenous and they are largely underrepresented in the political and economic arenas. Both MAS and MIP run on profound social reform platforms, which are similar to traditional patterns of organization already used on local levels by Aymara and Quechua communities. The established political parties formed by people of mostly European descent are nervous. They fear losing control of the government if the millions of Indian voters eventually decide to elect an indigenous president. Perhaps their fear will result in more consideration of the indigenous population in both governmental and economic policies.

RECENT GOVERNMENT ISSUES

Bolivia's government continues to struggle over a variety of issues that affect the country and its people. Instability, corruption, and a vast gap between those with power and the powerless are continuing problems. More recently, water and coca—two very important Bolivian resources—have become serious issues demanding attention.

The Water War

In 2000, during Hugo Banzer's last administration, a conflict that had simmered for months suddenly erupted in full flame. It was a conflict between the government and the country's poor. People were angry over a plan to privatize water and raise local water prices in the Cochabamba area. The government had signed a lucrative deal with foreign investors who would own and control Cochabamba's water and its prices. Residents of Cochabamba, joined by Bolivians in other parts of the country, protested violently, including setting up roadblocks. In Cochabamba, a city of 600,000, most of the population took to the streets to battle police and soldiers in what was called *la guerra del agua*, the Water War. Peasant farmers in nearby towns barricaded all roads into and out of the city, and several people were killed. President Banzer called a state of emergency. Eventually, the government was forced to withdraw from its contract with the United States-based Bechtel Corporation for the water rights. The unrest in Bolivia made many in the global water business nervous. Would citizens of other poor countries decide that water privatization was not in their best interest and revolt to secure the right to water?

The Coca War

As we have already seen, another issue affecting Bolivia is coca. The growing of coca has been an important part of Andean culture for centuries, but it is Bolivia's change toward growing coca meant for illegal cocaine production that has put the country in the international spotlight. In 1989, it was estimated that up to one-third of Bolivia's work force was dependent on the illegal production and trafficking of cocaine. In the 1980s, coca production for cocaine was the most lucrative of Bolivia's economic exports, generating an annual figure of US$1.5 billion. Half of this income remained in the country. Many of the miners laid off during Victor Paz Estenssoro's presidency turned to coca or cocaine as their main source of earnings. In the later 1980s, the United States began sending Drug Enforcement Agency (DEA) teams into the Beni Department and the Chapare region in the Cochabamba Department to begin coca eradication efforts. By the early 1990s, the United States threatened to end foreign aid unless Paz Estenssoro's government made efforts to end illegal cocaine production in the country. The president agreed to the eradication program proposed by the United States. Efforts by the Bolivian government, however, only seemed to organize the coca growers into increasingly powerful unions and interest groups. Profits from cocaine continued to grow during this time. This, coupled with corruption and poor law enforcement, resulted in increased cocaine production throughout Bolivia.

The Bolivian government refused to eradicate the coca

fields with chemicals and instead opted to pay each farmer US$2,000 per hectare (2.47 acres) to replace their coca crop with alternative crops such as bananas, coffee, yucca, cacao, and spices. As coca prices fell during the early 1990s, many farmers accepted the money and grew other crops. However, despite the millions of U.S. dollars spent to build processing plants for them, the markets for these goods were far away and transportation was difficult. Alternative crops simply could not provide the income possible with coca, which yields four harvests a year. As a result, many farmers took the money, then moved farther north to plant coca once again. Some farmers collected the $2,000 per hectare many times, only to continue producing coca in another location.

In 1990, President Jaime Paz Zamora asked the United States government for additional aid to be used in locating and arresting cocaine producers. U.S. President George H.W. Bush sent US$78 million and heightened activities in northern Bolivia as part of his "Operation Support Justice" campaign. The crackdown did not always pay off, though. In June 1991, Bolivian police and DEA agents executed a daylight helicopter raid on a small town north of Trinidad. They seized 15 cocaine labs, 9 estates, several private aircraft, and 243 pounds (110 kilograms) of cocaine base. But none of the traffickers were found.

By 1992, the DEA had increased its activity and secured a budget of US$21 billion to operate in South America. The United States feared two things with regard to Bolivia's drug war: that angry coca farmers or guerrilla factions would try to overthrow the government, and that corrupt military and government officials would misuse the millions of dollars allocated for the eradication efforts. U.S. military personnel stationed in the country also were concerned that much of the effort could be wasted. Over 85 percent of the Bolivian antinarcotic force (which only served one-year terms), after all, had family members involved in cocaine production. After their year of service ended, many used their U.S.-backed

In 1997, Bolivian military police patrolled the Chapare area looking for coca crops to destroy. In 1998, President Hugo Suarez Banzer took control of these eradication efforts and vowed to end all cocaine production by 2002. Despite these efforts, coca growing continues in Bolivia. As long as there is a demand for illegal drugs, this production can be expected to continue.

training to work as informants and sometimes guards to cocaine producers themselves.

By early 1995, the United States became impatient with the Bolivian government for its failure to destroy coca crops in a timely manner and set a deadline of June 30, 1995, for the eradication of 2,000 hectares (5,000 acres) of coca in the Chapare region, and another 3,500 hectares (8,650 acres) by December 31. It also demanded that Bolivia send captured cocaine producers and traffickers to the United States for trial. Bolivia met the June 30 deadline by paying farmers US$2,500 for each hectare destroyed. This put a heavy burden on Bolivian taxpayers, and not surprisingly many farmers just collected the money, changed locations, and began growing coca again.

Since 1995, the United States has continued to set deadlines for coca eradication in different regions of the country. At times, violence erupts over the eradication efforts. Many people, some of whom are innocent, have been arrested, or even killed, over the coca issue. Despite it all, the United States government is reluctant to consider that drug addiction and the resulting illegal trafficking is also a domestic problem.

In 1998, President Hugo Suárez Banzer took control of the coca eradication efforts. He ambitiously vowed to eradicate the entire coca crop in the Chapare region and all coca paste production by 2002. He also ended the program that compensated farmers for voluntary removal of coca crops; it was clearly failing to produce results.

The rights of coca growers, or *cocaleros*, have been championed by Evo Morales, the long-standing leader of the pro-coca movement. As mentioned earlier, Morales was elected to the Bolivian Congress in 1997 and nearly won the presidential election in 2002. Though he hasn't been able to make many direct changes benefiting the coca growers, his support appears to be growing.

Despite all the efforts by the U.S. and Bolivian governments, coca growing continues. Bolivian officials maintain that the amount of coca being grown is down in both the Chapare and Yungas regions. It seems likely, however, that as long as illegal drugs are in demand in the United States and elsewhere, and profits remain high for the cocaleros, Bolivia will continue to play an active role in the cocaine trade.

The old and the new coexist on the streets of La Paz. An Internet coffee shop (left) ties Bolivia to the global village.

CHAPTER

8

The Bolivian Economy

B olivia is a proud but very poor country. Currently, it has the second-lowest per capita income in South America, US$900 annually, slightly higher than that of Guyana. In 2001, Bolivia's gross domestic product (GDP) totaled US$8.4 billion.

No country in the world exceeds Bolivia's percentage of rural poverty. In fact, the International Fund for Agricultural Development says that 97 percent of Bolivia's rural population lives below the poverty line, and a World Health Organization representative once declared Bolivia to be poorer than Ethiopia. These data, however, do not tell the entire story.

As bad as the economic situation may seem, many rural Bolivians conduct their business outside the currency system and, therefore, have more "wealth" than is visible. Much of the rural population is composed of subsistence farmers, with sufficient farmland and livestock to provide an adequate, yet minimal lifestyle for their families.

Many factors have contributed to Bolivia's slow economic development. They include: a dominantly traditional (folk economy) society, political corruption, racism, international exploitation of natural resources, insufficient infrastructure, rugged terrain, and a lack of international markets to purchase Bolivian goods.

THE LABOR FORCE

Bolivia's total labor force is approximately 2.5 million people. Since there is a shortage of real jobs in Bolivia, many of the poorer people are part of the "informal sector." The informal sector consists of street trade, small stores and workshops, or personal services such as laundry, electrical, or mechanical repair services. Traditionally, it has also included those economic activities that fall outside the legal framework, such as the coca trade, illegal timber harvest, black market currency transactions, or the sale of smuggled consumer items. Transportation services, in the form of buses or taxis, are a popular and lucrative component of the informal sector. People have had to become very inventive and industrious in order to make money.

Out of economic necessity, the number of women workers in the informal sector has exploded. Women street sellers are common throughout Bolivia. Children are also working more often now, and subsequently the number of school dropouts is increasing. The expansion of the number of child workers is most evident in the larger cities. On the streets, shoeshine boys are seen with their faces covered, some say to avoid being recognized by their teachers. Often children are beggars, cigarette and candy sellers, or street musicians.

The formal labor sector consists mostly of professional workers. The best-paying jobs in the formal sector are in banking and oil and gas. Mining, education, and services, on the other hand, are paid the lowest wages. Skilled and semiskilled labor in Bolivia is scarce, and training is rare. Therefore, many people are unable to enter the formal labor sector.

The informal labor sector encompasses street trade, small stores and workshops, personal services such as laundry and electrical and mechanical repair services. Street vendors, such as this woman shown asleep on the streets of Copacabana, can be found in most, if not all, major cities and towns.

PRIMARY INDUSTRIES

A primary industry is one that utilizes land and resources. In Bolivia, the primary industries are agriculture, oil and gas extraction, mining, and forestry.

Agriculture

Most of Bolivia's agriculture is subsistence, grown to feed families rather than for sale. Agriculture contributes about 16 percent of the country's GDP and employs over a third of the population. In the highland areas, people grow mostly traditional crops for their own families, but surpluses may be sold at small local markets. Most of the crops consist of potatoes or grains, such as wheat, oats, barley, or quinoa. In addition to potatoes and grains, the valley areas are able to grow corn, cabbages, onions, garlic, carrots, and beets. The exportable crops of Bolivia are mainly grown on the fertile soils of the eastern lowlands. Here farmers are able to raise soybeans, sugar, cotton, and sunflowers (used for oil) for export to other countries. Soybeans are the most profitable legal cash crop in the country. In the lowlands, cultivation takes place on a much larger scale than in the highlands or valleys. Here, particularly in the Santa Cruz Department, foreign investors have created huge farming estates and processing plants. In the Yungas area, farmers also grow some coffee for export.

The most lucrative cash crop and economic activity in Bolivia is, of course, coca. In the lowland Chapare region, it is estimated that some 25,000 families grow coca on about 123,500 acres (50,000 hectares) of land. Growing and chewing coca is legal in Bolivia, but most of the coca in the Chapare is grown to make illegal cocaine for export. In 2001, the labor force employed in coca growing and illegal drug trafficking was about 350,000. It is estimated that the Chapare region yields up to 220,400 pounds (100,000 kilograms) of cocaine annually, and approximately US$350 million a year returns to Bolivia's economy from drug trafficking.

Petroleum and Natural Gas

Bolivia is focusing on oil and natural gas reserves for its economic future. These energy resources are found mostly in the eastern lowlands and they have replaced tin, gold, and silver as Bolivia's main natural resource exports. Natural gas has become one of the largest sources of legal export income, and it contributes nearly half of the total revenue. Bolivia is depending so heavily on oil and natural gas that it is currently helping build a 2,000-mile (3,150-kilometer) pipeline that will connect Santa Cruz with São Paulo, Brazil. The project will eventually cost US$1.9 billion.

Mining

Today, mining contributes only about 10 percent of Bolivia's GDP. The country has been hit hard by the decline of world tin markets, but it continues to be the world's leading tin producer. During Bolivia's recession in the 1980s, Comibol, the state-owned mining company, was forced to close most of its operations and lay off 23,000 miners. During the mid-1990s, Comibol sold its deposits, mines, smelters, and refineries. Mining may never create the economic boom it once did in Bolivia, but foreign investors are beginning to show an interest in gold mining, particularly near Oruro. Perhaps in the future, wealth from mining will return to Bolivia.

Forestry

The timber industry also contributes to Bolivia's GDP, though estimates say as much as 50 percent of all timber harvested is cut illegally. Income derived from this wood never enters the GDP. Though it is difficult to quantify the amount of timber being logged illegally, it is believed that all of it is sold domestically. Approximately 6.5 percent of Bolivia's total land area is currently being exploited legally for wood products. Private companies exploited about 14 million acres (5.7 million hectares) under government concessions, and indigenous groups log approximately 3.7 million acres (1.5 million hectares) under territorial land holdings. Practically all of this legal timber is exported to the United States, Europe, Chile, and Argentina. With illegal timber harvest factored into the equation, Bolivia may already be logging around 12 percent of its total land area.

SECONDARY INDUSTRIES

Secondary industries consist primarily of manufacturing activities that contribute to a country's economy. Manufacturing contributes less than 17 percent of Bolivia's GDP. Virtually the entire manufacturing sector is linked to the primary industries of agriculture, oil and gas, and mining. The goods produced by these primary industries must, however, be processed or manufactured for export.

Bolivia's manufacturing sector consists of nine subsectors: textiles, garments, and leather goods; food, beverages, and tobacco; chemicals and plastics; timber, wood products and furniture; paper products; equipment and machinery; nonmetallic minerals; basic metal industries; and metal production. The textile, food, and metal industries contribute over 80 percent of all manufacturing output and over half of the sector's labor force. Except for agricultural processing, most manufacturers are forced to import up to 90 percent of the raw materials that make up their final product.

In the agricultural processing sector, activities include packing meat, processing dairy products, canning fruits and vegetables, milling cotton into textiles, roasting coffee beans, refining sugar, crushing oilseeds, and milling wheat into flour. Domestic beverage manufacturers produce soft drinks, beer, and fruit juices. A thriving domestic cigar and cigarette industry also exists. The textile industry, while still a contributor to the manufacturing sector, has played a declining economic role in recent years. Though the mills are able to buy local cotton and wool for their products, the final garments, footwear, and leather goods are normally of poor quality. The textile subsector has also been undercut by smuggled or imported merchandise sold at cheaper rates.

The manufacturing sector also produces local gases, insecticides, chemicals, plastics, and medicines. As the gas pipeline from Bolivia to Brazil becomes operative, the manufacture of fertilizers and other petrochemicals will likely increase.

In the lowland areas, the timber industry is thriving, as more wood is being cut and sawmills are being built. Since the timber sector is often unregulated, illegal cutting and export occurs regularly. Brazil appears to be the country that benefits most from the felling of Bolivian trees. Bolivia's paper industry, which consists of several dozen companies producing paper goods, newsprint, and cardboard, also uses timber from the country's forests. Though Bolivia's timber industry is doing

This portable saw mill is shared by several communities to make lumber out of old hardwood trees. This initiative was funded by the "Big Tree" program run by the United States and the UN. This community could make about $9,000 in 3 months of 2002, in an area that formerly produced only coca for the illegal drug trade.

well, the wood and furniture industry has not been developed fully and seems to be below its potential.

Construction is also an important part of the manufacturing sector of the economy. This subsector mainly produces non-metallic minerals, such as limestone, clays, and salts to be used in construction activities. The cement industry is especially large, as construction of new houses and buildings increases in urban areas throughout Bolivia. The metal industry fabricates a wide range of goods, some of which are also used in construction. These include metal alloys, iron, steel, tubing, vehicles, some appliances, batteries, electrical transformers, sewing machines, farm equipment, bicycles, and transport equipment.

TERTIARY INDUSTRIES

Tertiary industries are those that provide services within a country. In Bolivia, the main tertiary industries are banking and financial services, transportation, communications, and tourism.

Banking and Financial Services

There are few banks in Bolivia. They are becoming more common in cities, where the affluent urban elite and other residents are beginning to use them. In the countryside, however, banks are still very rare and are not trusted by country folk. Rural campesinos usually choose to keep their money safely at home. In the rural areas, deals often are made through barter, or the exchange of goods. Agricultural lending institutions can be found in some of the larger towns. Farmers often solicit loans from these organizations to pay for seeds, fertilizer, or equipment, but the interest rates on loans are high. A family that has borrowed money can find itself in a desperate economic situation if the harvest is poor, markets are meager, or other extenuating circumstances arise, such as a hospital visit. The family might be unable to pay back the loan, but the interest continues to add up. As long as Bolivia's economy remains relatively stable, the banking industry should become an increasingly significant contributor of the country's economy.

Transportation

Over the years, poor transportation has constantly hindered Bolivia's growth and development. Though there is no shortage of automobiles, trucks, and buses, most roads are in poor condition. Approximately 1 percent of the country's roads are paved, some are cobblestones or gravel, but most are simple dirt tracks.

Surprisingly, almost every rural town and village has some form of transportation, either a large bus (*flota*), small bus (*micro*), or taxis, connecting it to the nearest major city. Some

Local people still transport goods by way of donkeys or llamas, but nearly every small town or village has bus or taxi transport for getting people around.

Indians in the highlands regions still use llamas or donkeys for the transportation of goods to markets. The railroad is important for transporting commodities to nearby countries, such as Chile, Argentina, and Brazil.

Air travel is common in Bolivia because of the poor roads and the physical topography that divides the country. For example, a bus trip from Cochabamba to Santa Cruz takes 12 hours and is normally hot and sticky, but a flight is only 35 minutes. In the eastern lowlands, river travel and transport is common.

Communications

The communications industry in Bolivia helps to unify people who are otherwise separated by many miles and rugged terrain. Telephone use is growing rapidly with over 350,000 telephone main lines in the country. Cellular telephone usage, especially in the cities, is also expanding. Nowadays, it is not uncommon to see urban teenagers using cell phones on buses, outside of universities, or on shopping trips.

Other communications industries are widespread. In 1999,

there were 171 AM, 73 FM, and 77 shortwave radio stations. Most of the radio stations are privately owned. It is estimated that over 5 million radios have access to programs broadcast in Spanish, Quechua, and Aymara. Over a million televisions receive programs from the approximately 50 television stations. Television is often one of the only links families in rural Bolivia have to the outside world.

Internet service has also come to Bolivia. Though the technology is still almost unheard of in rural towns, Internet cafes have sprung up on almost every street corner in major cities. Through Internet chat rooms, e-mail, and interactive games, Bolivian teenagers are able to connect with people in other parts of the country and the world. In the year 2000, hundreds of Internet cafes, nine Internet service providers, and 78,000 Internet users existed in Bolivia. These numbers continue to grow.

Tourism

Compared to most other Latin American countries, Bolivia has little tourist activity. Most people who do visit the country come to experience the wild natural beauty and unusual cultures. Popular attractions include Lake Titicaca, the Salar de Uyuni, the vast tropical areas, and the remote national parks. Very little of the tourism is domestic, though some more affluent Bolivians do travel for pleasure. The tourism industry is still in its formative stage and most development and promotion of tourism has been accomplished by private businesses, not the government. An estimated 600,000 tourists now visit the country each year. Most visitors are from Europe and elsewhere in the Americas. As the travel infrastructure—including highways and lodging and dining facilities—improves, the tourist industry will grow.

FOREIGN TRADE

Bolivian exports, which hit a low of US$652 million in 1991, rose to US$1.36 billion in 2001. Imports dropped slightly in 2001 to $1.72 billion. Bolivia negotiated several trade agreements in the last decade that increased its trading with neighboring countries. One of these is the Andean Community trade group. The group, which includes Peru, Ecuador, Colombia, and Venezuela, as well as Bolivia, allows virtually free trade between all the members. In 1997, Bolivia also joined MERCOSUR, the successful southern trading block, which aligned it with Argentina, Brazil, Paraguay, Uruguay, and Chile.

Most of Bolivia's trading is with the United States, which exported US$281 million worth of goods to Bolivia and imported US$182 million in 2001. Most of the merchandise exported to the United States from Bolivia includes tin, gold, jewelry, and wood products. Alpaca and llama products and some cotton textiles, which enter the United States on a duty-free basis, also are included in the exports. Bolivia, on the other hand, imports primarily computers, vehicles, wheat, and machinery.

FOREIGN ASSISTANCE AND DEBT

To finance development projects, Bolivia's government remains heavily dependent on foreign assistance. Bolivia owed US$4.4 billion to foreign creditors at the end of 2001. US$1.6 billion of this debt was owed to other governments, while the rest was owed to international development banks. Bolivia's most significant lenders are the International Monetary Fund (IMF) and the World Bank. Bolivia has a relatively good record of making payments to its creditors, although payments to other governments have been rescheduled on several occasions. When debt is rescheduled, the lender countries may apply very soft terms to the debt. In Bolivia's case, some countries have forgiven substantial amounts of the country's debt. As part of the Heavily Indebted Poor Countries (HIPC) debt relief programs, Bolivia's access to new soft loans is restricted.

In Oruro, which is approximately 143 miles (230 kilometers) from La Paz, these dancers represent native peoples of the Bolivian Amazon region during carnival celebrations on February 10, 2002.

9

Living in Bolivia Today

I n Bolivia, people's lives vary widely, depending mostly on geographic location and economic position. Some aspects of life, however, are inescapably the same throughout the country. For example, nearly everyone in Bolivia knows how to play *futbol*, known in the United States as soccer. And many of the holidays and festivals are either governmental or religious; hence, nearly everyone participates. A strong sense of national pride created by common traits helps bond most Bolivians together into a nation.

EDUCATION

Attendance in school (at least in theory) is required between the ages of 6 and 14. Today, public schools exist in or near all areas and communities. Generally, though, they are underfunded and of rather poor quality. Many wealthy families choose to send their children to private schools, most of which are church affiliated.

In rural areas, public school monies are nearly nonexistent, and teachers must often teach using whatever means possible. Sometimes a family cannot afford the school fees or supplies associated with an education. In fact, although 87 percent of Bolivia's children of primary school age are enrolled, attendance is often a low priority. Many times, youngsters stay home from school to help with chores, care for siblings or grandparents, or work selling goods or shining shoes. In fact, only about 40 percent of rural youngsters continue their education beyond the third grade. Public schools are now required to teach in both Spanish and the local language, but Bolivia's literacy rate of 80 percent continues to be dismal compared with other South American countries.

Major universities exist in Bolivia's largest cities. Though tuition is expensive for a middle-class family, more and more students are attending. They hope that higher education will give them a better chance at finding future employment.

HEALTH CARE

Today, most every large rural community in Bolivia has a health-care facility equipped to handle basic health problems. Some services are free, such as birth control and immunizations, but others cost a small fee. Even with an increased emphasis on health care in the past years, a huge gap still exists in the quality of health care available to people in rural and urban areas. Many rural people are hesitant to seek health care out of fear of medical staff and hospitals, concern over cost, or lack of knowledge about the severity of a health problem.

Infant mortality rates—a huge problem in Bolivia—vary regionally. Children living in the rural parts of the Altiplano, valleys, and Yungas regions have much higher mortality rates than those in the urban lowlands. Interestingly, infant mortality rates also differ among ethnic groups. They are highest among children of mothers who speak only native languages, are intermediate among bilingual mothers, and lowest among mothers who speak only Spanish. Measles, respiratory infections, or gastrointestinal diseases (such as those caused by parasites, giardia, or bacteria) cause approximately 80 percent of infant deaths. The lack of healthy diets, safe and clean water, and adequate sanitary facilities are the most common causes of these diseases.

LIVING CONDITIONS

Living conditions in Bolivia vary greatly region to region, or even town to town. Differences are based on such considerations as environment, culture, and economic status. Wealthy Bolivians usually live in cities, or in towns near cities. Their homes are large and more Western in style. Though they still may be built with the traditional adobe clay bricks, many homes have tile roofs. All cooking is done inside the home on a gas or electric stove. Most will have running water and indoor bathrooms. Many economic middle- and upper-class families have their own cars and may even visit McDonald's or Burger King, or shop at the supermarket. Many of these homes are gated to protect them from thieves. The people who are able to live in this manner in Bolivia, however, are in the minority; most of the population lives in relative poverty.

In general, poorer families living in rural or rural places have sparse accommodations. Their homes consist of locally available building materials and usually lack electricity and running water. They may even lack basic facilities such as latrines and kitchens. Cooking is done outside over a wood fire if there is no gas stove. Often these families, which can be quite large, share a one-room dwelling, and five or six people may even share a bed.

Chores are divided on the basis of gender and age. Mothers usually do all the cooking, clothes washing, and tending of children and livestock. Fathers are responsible for growing the

This stone hut above the city of Cochabamba lacks electricity and running water. In the distance one can see the large city of Cochabamba where many of the homes have modern amenities. Unfortunately, most of Bolivia's population lives in relative poverty.

crops. Mothers may occasionally help in the fields, especially at planting and harvesting time. Children may also help tend live-stock, watch after younger siblings, and help with the cooking. Meals normally consist of either leftovers, or tea and bread for breakfast, soup for lunch, and a dinner of the local staple, which is either potatos, rice, or *yucca* (cassava) with some type of meat.

While basic amenities exist for most families, there are regional differences in building materials and local diet. At higher elevations, people often construct their homes out of stone with straw roofs. Meals include potatoes (often *chuño*, a freeze-dried potato popular in the highlands) and meat, which usually comes in the form of llama jerky, called *charque*. In the highlands, it is important for people to have these dried staples on hand so that they can endure periods of drought and frost without lacking food. If available, other staples may include: *quesillo*, a goat-milk cheese; *choclo*, large boiled corn kernels; *habas*, fava beans; and eggs.

In the valleys region, people build their houses out of adobe (mud brick) huts and use straw or tin for the roofs. Meals in the valleys usually consist of potatoes, beef, chicken, or eggs, and may include vegetables, such as onions, carrots, and tomatoes. In general, food in the valleys is fresh and more varied because the area has a milder climate and longer growing season. Sometimes women in the valleys region will have added responsibilities, such as running a small store or a clothes-washing business.

In the lowlands, people normally live in wooden houses elevated on stilts to protect the home from flooding during the rainy season. Staples here include rice, yucca, and more fish, vegetables, and fruit.

FAMILY LIFE

Family life is very important in Bolivia. Regardless of the standard of living, extended families will often live near, or even next door, to one another. In the rural areas, three or four related men might farm the same piece of land, or a group of sisters, along with all of their children, might join to wash clothes together. Birthdays, weddings, and graduations are occasions for entire extended families to gather in celebration.

Doing chores becomes a social event when all the women in the family wash clothing in a stream.

Families tend to be large in Bolivia, so a grandmother and grandfather might have 20 or 25 grandchildren, making these gatherings joyous occasions.

FESTIVALS AND CELEBRATIONS

Fiestas are an important part of Bolivian life, and one that is hard to miss. They occur often and in every town. They may range from the large spectacle of *Carnaval* (Carnival) in the city of Oruro, to a simple llama sacrifice in a small town on the Altiplano in the hope of bringing a good harvest. Most festivals are related to Roman Catholic religious holidays, ancient pagan rituals, or political events, such as a battle, revolution, or independence. Fiestas can last from a few hours to 10 days and usually include plenty of ritual folk music, brass bands, food and drink, dancing, and parades. Depending on the fiesta, it may also include water balloon fights and fireworks.

Normally, the meaning of a fiesta is practical; people ask for a good harvest or fertile animals. Thus, the celebration is meant to give thanks to the sun and the rain, the fertile soils, and especially to Pachamama, the most sacred of all native gods. People wear brightly colored traditional costumes and dance throughout the night. Whenever drinking is involved, people are sure to pour a little on the ground as a sacrifice to Pachamama. Many costumes and dances associated with fiestas are derived from characters in popular Bolivian myths. Some date to colonial times, but have Tiahuanacan or Incan roots.

Carnaval is the most famous fiesta. Although it is celebrated throughout the country, the most famous event is in Oruro. Carnaval occurs the week before Lent (usually in February or March) and lasts about a week. It begins with the *entrada*, a huge parade that is the fiesta's featured event. In Oruro, the 3.1-mile (5-kilometer) entrada begins at 7:00 in the morning and over 50 dance groups participate. *La Diablada* (the Dance of the Devils) and *La Morenada* (the Dance of the Black Slaves) are the most important dances. La Diablada is led by a condor and dancing apes and bears. Archangel Michael chases Satan and Lucifer, dressed in diabolical costumes and followed by their band of female dancing demons. Behind the initial Diablada come 50 or more groups, including more Diabladas, each with its own band.

La Morenada represents the black slaves who were brought to Bolivia during the colonial period and sent to work in the mines of Potosí. The richly decorated costumes are meant to symbolize the wealth of the slaveowners. The protruding tongues and eyes of the masks, on the other hand, signify the pain and suffering endured by the slaves from altitude sickness. Two days after the entrada, a dance competition between the *Diablos* and *Morenos* takes place in the streets of Oruro.

ARTS

Although the Spanish succeeded in destroying much of Bolivia's artistic heritage, Bolivians have adapted and evolved their traditions using both European techniques and materials, as well as their own ancient methods. Today, whether in weaving, traditional music, or dance, Bolivians have a flair for creating beauty.

Weaving, Knitting, and Spinning

Bolivian weaving and spinning traditions have changed little in thousands of years. To the Incas, only humans and llamas were more important than textiles in people's lives. In many communities, older weavings are still passed down from generation to generation. In some cases, sadly, economic hardship has forced families to sell their most prized weavings to foreigners. Ancient weaving traditions are being lost in many areas. Increased use of modern weaving methods, many using machines, destroys the traditional art form.

In rural areas, young girls learn how to weave and knit usually before they reach puberty. Women often spend much of their free time spinning llama, alpaca, or sheep wool on small handheld drop spindles. It is very common to see women walking or herding their animals while spinning wool. When they have enough wool, they may dye it wonderful colors created from natural products, such as plants, bark, or an insect larva that produces a bright fuchsia color. Then they either knit or weave it into masterful textiles for family members or for sale. Looms are often large and bulky, sometimes eight feet in length, and are always handmade from wood of local trees.

Bolivian weavings vary regionally and some are much more detailed than others. An extremely detailed weaving, with over 50 threads per centimeter, can take 6 months or more to complete. These weavings are truly functional, beautiful works of art, and the designs are usually very symbolic to the weaver.

Some of the more common items woven in Bolivia are the *chuspa*, a small bag used by men to carry coca leaves, the *axsu*, a rectangular overskirt worn by women, or the *aguayo*, a multiuse piece of fabric worn over the shoulders and used to carry everything from babies to potatoes.

Knitting is more recent than weaving in Bolivia, but women do knit lovely sweaters, hats, and scarves. They normally create these knitted pieces for family members. Increasingly, however, knitting and weaving cooperatives are beginning to appear. These co-ops buy the handmade goods and sell them to international traders.

In some areas, especially in the Department of Chuquisaca near the city of Sucre, men also have a tradition of weaving and knitting. Though their textiles look very different than those crafted by women, they are just as beautiful and colorful and often depict animals.

MUSIC AND DANCE

Bolivia's music and dance traditions, like many other aspects of the culture, differ from region to region. When people think of "Andean music," it is most likely that the haunting instrumentals of the highland Quechua and Aymara Indians come to mind. The most common instruments used in this type of music are the guitar, the *charango* (a tiny stringed instrument similar to a ukulele), and the *zampoña* (a flute made of reeds). Percussion instruments also may be included. Today, some musicians are adding appropriately tragic, sorrowful words to these melodic tunes from the Altiplano. The most popular Bolivian group is Los Kjarkas. They have been playing traditional Andean music for over 25 years and have a large international following.

Today, most of the recorded music heard in urban areas is mainstream. The most popular type is *cumbia*, which is Colombian in origin. It consists of Latin rhythms mixed with synthesized sounds. Bolivian people especially like to dance to cumbia, and it can be heard on outside speakers at restaurants and on most radio stations. Music from the United States or Europe is also popular. Even though lyrics are in English and cannot be understood by most listeners, young people flock to buy pirated CDs on the streets of most cities.

Bolivians love to dance. At practically every fiesta, graduation, wedding, or even small get-together, someone brings music and dancing follows. The most popular dance is the *cueca*, a whirling dance between handkerchief-waving couples. The dance originated in Spain as the *fandango*, but the Bolivian cueca is a Creole adaptation brought from Chile. The cueca tells a story of courtship, love, lost love, and reconciliation between a man and a woman. The dance itself is loosely defined, but the man normally circles the woman numerous times. The audience is also included through clapping and shouts of "*aro, aro, aro*" at strategic moments.

Many other dances are performed throughout Bolivia. The *chapaqueada*, for example, is a dance famous in Tarija and throughout the southern part of the country. It is usually danced at religious festivals, such as Christmas and Easter. This dance is usually accompanied by a host of unusual instruments found in Tarija.

The *auqui-auqui*, or "old man" dance of the Altiplano is meant to satirize Spanish colonial gentlemen. The dancers carry sticks, have flowing beards and long, pointed noses, and wear top hats. They dance around in a stooped position to exaggerate their ages. Copious other indigenous and Spanish-influenced dances can be found in every region of the country.

RECREATION AND SPORTS

Just as with festivals and dancing, sports and recreation are vital in the lives of most Bolivian people. The most common sport known to almost every Bolivian is futbol. Children play futbol in school for exercise, women's groups have futbol tournaments on International Women's Day and Mothers Day, and men often play on teams sponsored by different groups in the community. Practically every rural community has an open dirt field dedicated to futbol. Most Sundays will find nearly every member of the community around the soccer field watching his or her favorite team play.

Each Bolivian city has at least one national team that plays other teams around the country and some engage in competition with teams from other South American countries. Although these teams from Bolivia aren't exactly international futbol powerhouses, they do very well against some of the best teams in the world, such as Brazil and Argentina, when they play in Bolivia. Visitors find it very difficult to play in the rarified atmosphere found at elevations of over 12,000 feet (3,658 meters)!

Other popular sports in Bolivia include *fubito*, volleyball, basketball, and racquetball. Fubito is similar to soccer but is played on a much shorter cemented court with small goals on either end. The ball is also about half the size of a regular soccer ball without much bounce. The game can be rough, as space is limited, but it is very entertaining to watch because it moves very quickly. Volleyball, basketball, and racquetball are relatively new sports to Bolivia but are enjoyed by both men and women.

Although Bolivians, especially in the rural areas, spend much of their time working, they can usually make time for their families on Sundays. Sunday is the unofficial "family day" in Bolivia. People usually spend the day watching or playing futbol, eating *chicharron* (slow-cooked pig), drinking chicha, and dancing the cueca until all hours of the night. Bolivians just love to have fun—particularly with their families.

In June 1998, children try out Microsoft Windows 98 operating system at a computer store in the Chijini neighborhood of La Paz.

10

Bolivia Looks to the Future

B olivia has the potential to become a strong and stable country. It is rich in human and natural resources. However, the country must work hard if it is to overcome some of its obstacles and achieve its goals for the future. During almost 300 years of Spanish colonial rule, extreme imbalances in wealth and power have occurred between Bolivia's conquered Indians and Spanish elite. These imbalances produced unstable and unequal political, economic, and social conditions for many people. Such conditions continue to exist in Bolivian society, but Bolivians have reason to be hopeful about their future.

The country contains a wealth of natural resources. It has large stores of petroleum and natural gas and also rich deposits of gold, silver, iron, and tin. If used wisely, these riches can provide a much needed boost to the economy. Bolivia contains an abundance of cultural, historical, and natural attractions, and tourism is slowly growing throughout the country. However, Bolivia's eight million people may be its most valuable resource of all. They are strong, proud, hard-working, family-oriented, and eager to make Bolivia a better place to live.

Bolivia does face some challenges, though. As we have seen, over 97 percent of its rural population still lives in extreme poverty. To overcome this huge problem, the country must advance in many ways. The government must take responsibility for initiating most of the changes needed to make a difference in the life of the average Bolivian.

First, corruption within the government must cease. Bolivians will have to elect a president and members of Congress who sympathize with the indigenous population and want to make life better for all of the country's poor.

Second, the educational system will have to improve. The Bolivian government will have to put more emphasis on education for its rural poor and pledge more money to meeting educational needs. Having an educated and literate population is essential if the country is to develop economically.

Third, the government should increase the economic opportunities for its people by engaging in world markets. Though this phase must be undertaken with care to protect both the natural environment and Bolivia's people, the country could definitely profit from increased international economic activity. Bolivia has the potential to export hundreds of value-added products (those products made in Bolivia from start to finish, with only Bolivian materials) and provide much-needed revenue to governmental programs that benefit all of society.

Fourth, the government must take care to prevent increased drug trafficking. Not only does the drug trade pose a problem by possibly limiting a country's foreign aid, it can also leave the country vulnerable to rule by dangerous military juntas and guerrillas.

The government is also faced with serious environmental

problems. It must recognize the value of Bolivia's incredible natural resources and pass legislation to protect them. Stiff penalties should be posed to guard against illegal timber harvest, mineral extraction, and wildlife poaching. It will be important in the future to heighten vigilance in this respect, not only for the sake of environmental protection itself, but also as a means of investing in a fledgling local industry—tourism. The government is also challenged to discover a solution to the air, water, and land pollution created by automobile and factory emissions, garbage disposal, and now-abandoned mining operations. Bolivia must continue educating farmers of the need for soil, water, and vegetation conservation. In essence, the government must step up its action in environmental management and restoration if Bolivia is to remain beautiful and productive for years to come.

To effect positive social change and help lessen poverty throughout Bolivia, the people themselves must be responsible for ending any prejudice and discrimination that exists between and among different groups.

Although Bolivia has many obstacles to overcome, it has great potential. To achieve this potential, it is essential that the country have strong, honest, responsive government leadership. All segments of Bolivian society also must work together toward achieving the goal of a strong and vibrant nation.

Facts at a Glance

Land and People

Official Name	Republic of Bolivia
Location	In Central South America, bordered by Peru to the northwest, Chile to the southwest, Brazil to the north and east, Paraguay to the southeast, and Argentina to the south
Area	424,164 square miles (1,098,580 square kilometers)
Climate	Climate varies with altitude; from cold and semiarid in the mountains and Altiplano to humid and tropical in the eastern lowlands
Capital	La Paz (seat of government); Sucre (legal capital and seat of judiciary)
Other Cities	Cochabamba, Santa Cruz de la Sierra, El Alto
Population	8,445,134 (July 2002)
Population Distribution	Rural, 38 percent; urban, 62 percent
Major Rivers	Río Beni and its main affluent, the Río Madre de Dios; the Rio Guaporé, which forms part of the boundary with Brazil; and the Río Mamoré
Mountains	Illimani, Sajama, Huayna Potosí
Highest Point	Sajama, 21,420 feet (6,529 meters)
Official Languages	Spanish, Quechua, Aymara
Other Languages	Approximately 30 languages spoken mostly by low-lands indigenous groups, of which Guaraní is the most populous
Ethnic Groups	Quechua, 30 percent; Aymara, 23 percent; mestizo, 30 percent; people of European origin, 15 percent; others (including Guaraní, Ayoreo, Chiquitano, Chiriguano, Guaravo, Chimane, Mojo, Chipaya, and Uru), 2 percent
Religions	Roman Catholic, 95 percent; Protestant (Evangelical), unknown
Literacy Rate	80 percent
Average Life Expectancy	females, 67.1 years; males, 61.86 years

Economy

Natural Resources	Petroleum, natural gas, timber, minerals such as tin, antimony, bismuth, silver, lead, zinc, gold, potassium, lithium, and iron

Agricultural Products	Soybeans, coffee, coca, cotton, corn, sugarcane, rice, potatoes timber
Industries	Mining, smelting, petroleum, food and beverages, tobacco, handicrafts, clothing
Major Imports	Capital goods, raw materials and semimanufactures, chemicals, petroleum, food
Major Exports	Soybeans, natural gas, zinc, gold, wood
Currency	Boliviano

Government

Form of Government	Republic
Governmental Bodies	Formal executive, legislative, and judicial branches
Formal Head of State	President
Administrative Divisions	Nine departments (states): Chuquisaca, Cochabamba, Beni, La Paz, Oruro, Pando, Potosi, Santa Cruz, Tarija

7000–8000 B.C.	Archaeological evidence found on the Altiplano indicates the presence of humans in Bolivia.
3000 B.C.	People living in the Lake Titicaca area begin to participate in intensive agriculture and herding.
500–1200 A.D.	The southernmost of the pre-Columbian Andean empires, the Tiahuanaco, expands into and rules the areas surrounding Lake Titicaca and beyond.
1100–1500	The Tiahuanaco Empire disappears; several different Aymara kingdoms take over and dominate the central highlands of Bolivia.
1450–1600	The Incas, who are mostly Quechua people, colonize a vast area stretching from north of the equator to central Chile, including present-day Bolivia.
1542	The Spanish arrive, conquer, and annex present-day Bolivia into what is called the Audencia of Charcas of the Viceroyalty of Peru.
1545	The Bolivian city of Potosí is founded and massive exploitation of minerals utilizing indigenous slave labor begins on Cerro Rico.
1545–1825	As many as eight million Indians and Africans die from the horrible conditions in the mines at Potosí.
1569–1767	Jesuit priests form communities in the eastern lowlands of Bolivia; the missionaries promote cultural and educational development among the Indians while also converting them to Catholicism.
1825	August 6: With the help of Simón Bolívar, Bolivia wins its independence from Spain.
1879–1884	Bolivia loses the War of the Pacific against Chile; the country's only outlet to the sea is lost.
1903	Bolivia loses the war with Brazil, the remote Arce territory in the eastern lowlands, and plenty of rubber trees.
1900–1920	Tin emerges as the most important mineral resource for Bolivia.
1932–1935	Substantial loss to Paraguay in the Chaco War; 55,000 men and a sizeable amount of land lost.
1940s	A new nationalist political party, the Movimiento Nacionalista Revolucionario (MNR), or National Revolution Movement, is started; its political influence continues for the next 60 years.

1952	The Bolivian National Revolution occurs when miners, police, peasants, urban factory workers, and members of the lower middle class fight a military junta and win.
1953	The government sets up the Agrarian Reform Program that redistributes lands held by wealthy landowners to peasant farmers.
1960s–1990s	The political scene is marked by successive corrupt and unstable governments.
1987–2002	United States Drug Enforcement Agency (DEA), coupled with the Bolivian government, attempts to eradicate all coca growing for cocaine production.
2000	Riots ensue throughout the country over the privatization of water utilities in Cochabamba by a U.S. private investment firm; the government finally concedes and abandons the contract.
2002	Evo Morales, the leader of the coca growers' movement, places second behind Gonzalo Sanchez de Lozada in presidential elections; Bolivia's indigenous population considers it a major victory.

Bibliography

Anstee, Margaret Joan. *Gate of the Sun: A Prospect of Bolivia*. London: Longman, 1970.

Carter, William. *Bolivia: A Profile*. New York: Praeger Publishers, 1971.

U.S. Central Intelligence Agency. *The World Factbook—Bolivia*. (http://www.cia.gov/cia/publications/factbook/geos/bl.html).

Federal Research Division of the Library of Congress. Hudson, Rex A. and Hanratty, Dennis M., eds. *Bolivia: A Country Study*. Washington, D.C.: Library of Congress, 1991.

Klein, Herbert S. *Bolivia: The Evolution of a Multi-Ethnic Society*. New York: Oxford University Press, 1982.

Murphy, Alan. *Bolivia Handbook*. Bath, England: Footprint Handbooks, 2000.

Swaney, Deanna. *Bolivia*. Melbourne: Lonely Planet Publications, 2001.

U.S. Department of State. *Background Notes–Bolivia*. (http://www.state.gov/r/pa/ei/bgn/1958.htm).

Bigenho, Michelle. *Sounding Indigenous.* Houndmills, England: Palgrave Macmillan Ltd., 2002.

Davis, Wade. *One River: Explorations and Discoveries in the Amazon Rain Forest.* New York: Touchstone, 1996.

Gill, Lesley. *Teetering on the Rim.* New York: Columbia University Press, 2000.

Ghinsberg, Yossi. *Back from Tuichi: The Harrowing Life-And-Death Story of Survival in the Amazon Rainforest.* New York: Random House, 1993.

Guevara, Ernesto, and James, Daniel. *The Complete Bolivian Diaries of Ché Guevara, and Other Captured Documents.* Lanham, Maryland: Cooper Square Press, 2000.

Kolata, Alan. *Valley of the Spirits : A Journey Into the Lost Realm of the Aymara.* New York: John Wiley & Sons, 1996.

Lehman, Kenneth Duane. *Bolivia and the United States: A Limited Partnership (The United States and the Americas).* Athens, Georgia: University of Georgia Press, 1999.

Nash, June. *We Eat the Mines and the Mines Eat Us: Dependency and Exploitation in Bolivian Tin Mines.* New York: Columbia University Press, 1993.

Index

Index

Index

Index

Picture Credits

About the Authors

MANDY LINEBACK GRITZNER and **JASON M. GRITZNER** recently returned from Cochabamba, Bolivia, where they worked in natural resource conservation and environmental education as United States Peace Corps volunteers. Mandy holds a Master of Science degree in Earth Science from Montana State University and Jason holds a Master of Science degree in Natural Resources Conservation from the University of Montana. They reside with daughter Maya Rose and dog Jaspur east of Lassen National Park, California, where Jason is employed by the U.S. Forest Service as a hydrologist for the Lassen National Forest. They both enjoy mountain biking, snowboarding, and traveling.

CHARLES F. ("FRITZ") GRITZNER is Distinguished Professor of Geography at South Dakota University in Brookings. He is now in his fifth decade of college teaching and research. During his career, he has taught more than 60 different courses, spanning the fields of physical, cultural, and regional geography. In addition to his teaching, he enjoys writing, working with teachers, and sharing his love for geography with students. As consulting editor for the MODERN WORLD NATIONS series, he has a wonderful opportunity to combine each of these "hobbies." Fritz has served as both president and executive director of the National Council for Geographic Education and has received the Council's highest honor, the George J. Miller Award for Distinguished Service.